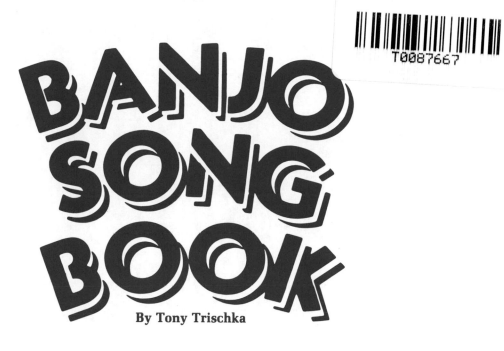

BANJO SONG BOOK

By Tony Trischka

Oak Publications
New York / London

PHOTOGRAPHS

Page	Photographer
30	John Lee
33	Carl Fleischhauer
36	Carl Fleischhauer
42	Henry Horenstein
46	Carl Fleischhauer
51	David Gahr
57	Freida Jensen
59	Courtesy of the John Edwards Memorial Foundation
62	John Lee
68	Mark Sukoenig
73	Mark Sukoenig
99	Harumi Itoh
107	Carl Fleischhauer (bottom right)
	Phil Straw (bottom left)
	Jack Tottle (top)

Cover design by Iris Weinstein
Book design by Mark Stein

Order No. OK 63438
International Standard Book Number: 0.8256.0197.5
Library of Congress Catalog Card Number: 76-51890

© 1977 by Oak Publications,
A Division of Embassy Music Corporation, New York, NY.

Exclusive Distributors:
Music Sales Corporation
257 Park Avenue South, New York, NY 10010 USA
Music Sales Limited
8/9 Frith Street, London W1V 5TZ England
Music Sales Pty. Limited
120 Rothschild Street, Rosebery, Sydney NSW 2018 Australia

Printed in the United States of America by
Vicks Lithograph and Printing Corporation

Dedication

To the Banjoists of America,
And to those who are learning;
To those who aspire to the higher art—
To those within whom the Light is burning.
(That Light which lends to human beings the power of the Gods)
And to those who for greater knowledge are yearning.
To one and all, both rich and poor;
To the man of gall,—the unconscious boor.
To the little ones—ofttimes called great;
And also to those who the Banjo hate.
To the poor, because the book is cheap,
To the rich, because the volume's neat—
To him who reads and reading thinks;
To him who presses onward—never sinks.
To every student who wishes to learn,
And to all who perchance would attention turn
To THE BANJO, this little volume is faithfully inscribed, by

S. S. STEWART
Philadelphia, August, 1888
(from *The Banjo* by S. S. Stewart)

This book is dedicated with love to the following people:

My family—John and Aurora Trischka and to the memory of my mother, Coryl Trischka

Peter and Nondi Wernick—for their warmth and strength and, in particular, to Peter for giving me the opportunity to write

Debra Schwartz Avidan—for giving me the happiest month of my life

Bela Fleck—for his valued friendship and for transcribing most of the tablature in this book

Danny Weiss and Rosemary Dunlap—for being their sunny selves

Dorothy Hughes—for following her own path and giving so generously

everyone involved with the Robber Bridegroom—for a wonderful run

Randy McNamara, Werner Erhard and est—for creating so much space.

Thanks also go to the following people who assisted in the preparation of this book:

Hank Sapoznik—for daring to undertake the Herculean task of writing out all of the tablature found on these pages

Alan Kaufman—for teaching me a good number of the fiddle tunes in this book and for being a selfless psychic editor

Beth Goldman—for typing the manuscript and for giving me insight at important times

Tim Newcomb—for his fine illustrations

Doug Tuchman—for setting up my interviews with Don Reno and Snuffy Jenkins

The Staff at Oak—Jason Shulman, Judy Hinger, Iris Weinstein, Barbara Hoffman, Stuart Isacoff, and Mark Stein—for their friendship and support, and all of the musicians who shared themselves with me in the interviews.

The fine people at the John Edwards Memorial Foundation—Paul Wells, Michael Mendelson and Rebecca Ziegler for their kind assistance.

Contents

Introduction

When I first started playing the banjo back in 1962, tablature was at a premium. Pete Seeger's book had a couple of Scruggs tunes in it and that was about it. If you wanted to learn anything you had to have either a teacher or a good ear for picking up breaks off of records.

In recent years, though, there's been a boom in banjo books. Most have concentrated on instruction. This one, however, has as its fundamental purpose the expansion of the basic banjo repertoire. It *is* a songbook, filled with fiddle tunes, bluegrass songs, classical pieces and, of course, some down to earth banjo breakdowns. For those of you who are beginners, the book will provide a wide new space for you to work out of. An instructional section early on will explain all of the techniques you'll need to handle anything that comes up in this book. Also, you'll see your playing improve simply in the process of working through the tunes. Since they range from easy to more difficult in each section, you should start somewhere near the beginning and work your way outward from there. If you're a more experienced player, you'll find fresh arrangements for many of the familiar tunes plus a goodly number of new pieces.

Although I originally intended this to be strictly a songbook, it gradually took on aspects of a history book as well. I've traced the development of the three-finger style from the classic approach of the 1860s, through the old time styles of the 1920s and 30s, right up to the progressive styles of today. I've combined songs, interviews and musical examples to flesh out the musical lives of such prime movers as Fred Van Epps, Charlie Poole, Snuffy Jenkins, Earl Scruggs, Don Reno, Ralph Stanley, Bill Keith, Butch Robins and Larry McNeely. I had always felt there was a connecting thread that ran through the styles of these men, a feeling that proved to be true as I wrote the book. There was a real excitement for me in that discovery. I also had the opportunity to talk with many of the people who influenced me and to whom I am very grateful. There would have been nothing to write about without them.

So, you see, what you have here is really two books in one. I hope you receive as much value reading and playing through them as I did in putting them together.

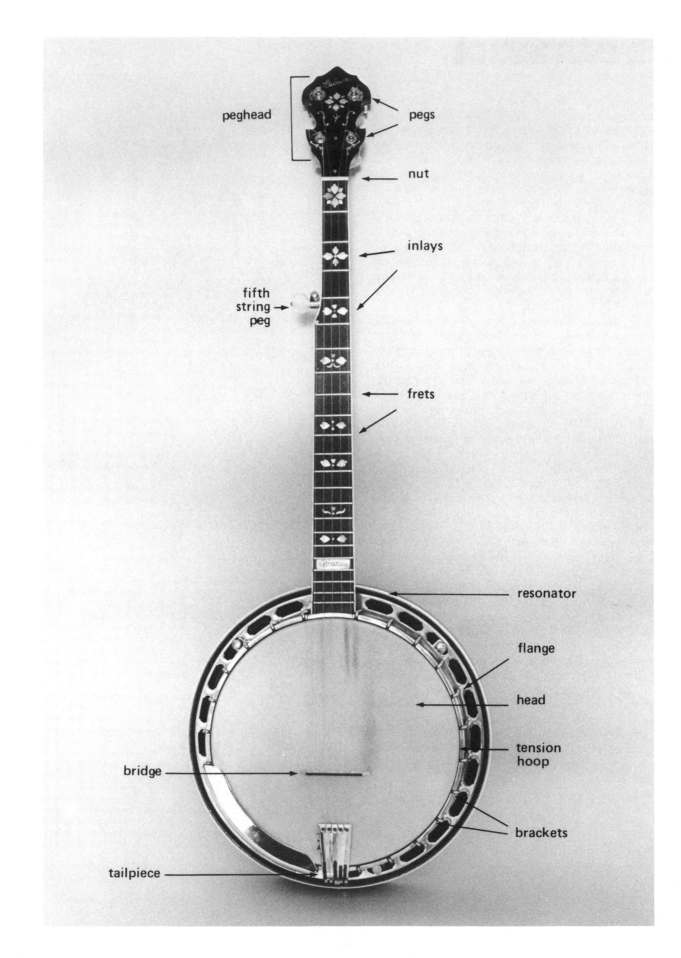

peghead

pegs

nut

inlays

fifth
string
peg

frets

resonator

flange

head

tension
hoop

bridge

brackets

tailpiece

Tuning

Before you do anything else, make sure you're in tune. There are several ways to do this, the first of which involves tuning to a piano. Here's how the strings of the banjo relate to the keys of the piano.

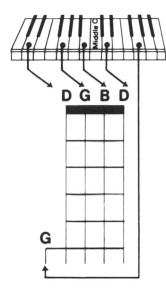

As you can see, you have three basic notes to work with—G, D, and B. Play one of these, say the lower G, on the piano, and check it with the comparable string on the banjo. If the G on the banjo is a little bit higher *(sharp)* or slightly lower *(flat)* when compared to the piano note, simply adjust the tuning peg for the third string until both notes are in sync. Then do the same for the rest of the strings. While doing all of this, you should be continually picking the string you are tuning so that you can keep track of where you are tonally in relation to the piano.

Now, if you live in a fifteen floor walk-up, you probably won't have a piano, in which case you'll have to tune to something else, such as a guitar or tuning fork. If you want to tune to a guitar, have the other person (who is presumably already in tune) play his or her G note, and tune your open third string to it. Once you've done that you can use the following method to get the rest of your notes in tune.

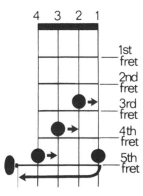

Match the fifth fret of the fourth string with the open third string (G).

Match the fourth fret of the third string with the open second string.

Match the third fret of the second string with the open first string.

Match the fifth fret of the first string with the open fifth string.

If you're interested in using a tuning fork (which is always in tune), you'll find that most music stores sell G forks, which will produce the G note you need. Holding the handle of the tuning fork in your right hand, strike the fork end against your knee or the top of your head (if your skull isn't too fragile), and place the end of the handle on the bridge. The vibrations of the fork will be transmitted through the bridge to the head of the banjo, thus amplifying the G to the point where it will ring out clearly. Once you have that note in your head, tune the open third string to it and then use the method mentioned above to tune the rest of your banjo.

If you're really out of tune when you start, or if you're putting on a new set of strings, you may find that by the time you get the last string in tune, the first one will be out of tune again. This results from a change in the distribution of tension on the head—created by tuning. When this happens, don't get frustrated: just go through the tuning process one more time, and finish off the minor adjustments.

Now we can go on.

Picks

When you get ready to play with other people, you'll want to be sure your banjo can cut across the sound of the other instruments so that your breaks can be heard. That will only be possible if you're using fingerpicks. Most people favor two metal fingerpicks (National or Dunlop work fine) and a plastic thumbpick.

Since the fingerpicks are adjustable, there's no reason to make them so tight that the tips of your fingers turn blue. By the same token, they shouldn't be so loose that they fly into the audience in the middle of a hot tune.

Another thing to watch out for is your initial reaction to wearing finger picks. When I first started playing, I found them tremendously distracting. They felt strange, and managed to create an awful lot of extraneous metallic sound as they hit the strings. After a few days, though, they became a natural extension of my fingers. So just stay with them. They're necessary.

Left Hand Position

You should cradle the neck of the banjo between your thumb and fingers. Be sure you're not pressing down too hard on the neck. Your left hand should be fairly relaxed. Also, keep your fingers poised fairly closely over the strings. This will give you an extra measure of speed, because your fingers will have less distance to travel to get down to the fretboard.

Another thing to watch out for: Whether you're fingering backup chords or playing flat out, you should always keep your fingers fairly close to the frets.

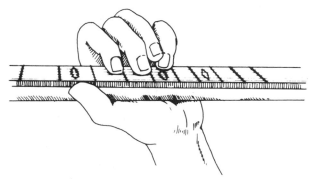

If your fingers are hanging out more midway between the frets, you run a greater risk of creating string buzz.

Right Hand Position

If you check out the parking lot pickers at the next bluegrass festival you attend, you'll probably see a variety of right hand positions being used. The most common of these (and the one I consider to be most beneficial) involves planting the pinky and ring finger on the banjo head on the neckward side of the bridge. This will give you the most support for hard-driving playing, as well as the clearest, most bell-like tone. You can experiment with the distance between the two planted fingers and the bridge, depending on the kind of sound you want to get out of your banjo. If you're looking for a harder, more piercing sound (à la Ralph Stanley), move closer to the bridge. For a mellower tone, move more in the direction of the neck (this position is also good for backup playing). Generally, though, if you keep about half an inch between your pinky and the bridge, you'll be in good shape.

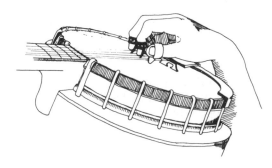

As you can see, your hand should be slightly arched at the wrist. Also you should be picking pretty much straight up on the strings, as opposed to coming at them from an angle.

Remember, correct positioning of the right hand is crucial to getting a good sound out of your instrument.

A Word on Tablature

Most bluegrass players don't read standard musical notation. For this reason, tablature has become the popular means of transmitting bluegrass music from the printed page to the mind and fingers of the picker.

Briefly, tablature is a simple method of notation which applies only to the instrument for which it is written. It had its initial heyday between the fifteenth and seventeenth centuries, and was used mostly in writing for lute, viol (fretted violin), and organ. Although the popularity of tablature faded in the eighteenth century, the folk and bluegrass boom of recent times has given it a new home in the twentieth.

The *tab* in this book uses a five line *staff*—one line for each string of the banjo.

The vertical bars divide the staff into equal sections called *measures*. The length of each measure is determined by the *time signature* of the entire tune. The time signature is the 2/4, 3/4, 6/8, and so on, that you see in the first measure of a piece written in standard musical notation. The bottom number refers to the value of the note: 4 = *quarter note*, 8 = *eighth note*, and so forth. The top number refers to the number of those notes per measure. Most of the tunes in this book are in 2/4 time, which signifies that there are two quarter notes per measure. The dark slashes represent downbeats, and the light slashes, upbeats.

The equivalent is four *eighth notes*

or eight *sixteenth notes* per measure.

This last example is the one we'll come in contact with most often in the pages to come.

Now, instead of actual notes, tablature places numbers on the staff to indicate the fret and string to be fingered by the left hand. For instance, this

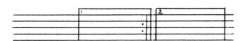

translates into the third fret of the second string. An *O* means that the string should be played open, and an *X* on the third string refers to a sixteenth-note rest (or a space where no note is played).

Here is how tablature indicates which finger of the right hand will pick a particular note:

T = thumb
1 = index finger
2 = middle finger

Here's an example which combines the various elements mentioned above.

Repeat Sign

Many of the tunes in this book, especially the fiddle tunes, are in an AABB form—in other words, in two repeating parts. In order to save time and space when writing these out in tab, repeat signs are used.

The signs ╟ and ╢ indicate that the section enclosed by them should be repeated. If the section to be repeated has two separate endings, it will be notated like this:

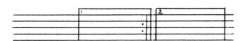

This means that you should play through the entire section once, including the first ending. Then return to the beginning and play through the section again, this time skipping the first ending, and playing the second.

Triplets

Triplets will appear from time to time in the tablature—most often in the fiddle tunes—and are notated like this:

A triplet consists of three notes, crammed into the time value of two. In our case, we'll be dealing with sixteenth note triplets that are equivalent to two sixteenth notes. This may sound confusing, but the following example should help clarify things.

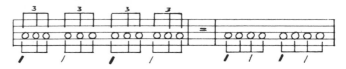

For a healthy dose of triplets, check the *A* part of "Galway Hornpipe."

P.S. When you start to write out your own tab, remember that standard music notation also uses a five-line staff. So instead of spending undue amounts of time drawing your own lines, you can simply pick up some music paper at your local music store.

Basic Chord Positions

After you've been playing for a short while, you'll realize that the G position is your best bet for getting a driving, wide-open, bluegrass sound. For that reason, you should start off by learning the three most commonly used chords in the key of G: G, C, and D.

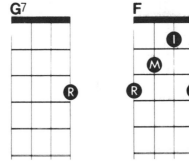

You can also call these I, IV, and V chords, respectively. These numbers refer to the chords that are built around the first, fourth, and fifth notes of any scale you're playing. (See Appendix 1 for more details.) In the key of C, the I, IV, and V chords are C, F, and G7.

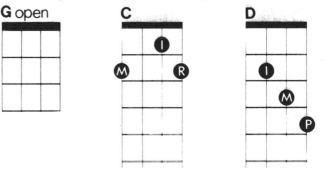

Most bluegrass—in fact, the majority of western music—is based on the I, IV, V chord progression. Musicians often use these numbers instead of letter names because it's the fastest way to communicate chord changes.

This next chart, taken from Peter Wernick's Oak publication, *Bluegrass Banjo*, lists all of the important chords in the seven major keys, including the II, VI, and VII chords.

Keys

	I	IV	V	II	VI	VII
A	A	D	E	B	F#	G
B	B	E	F#	C#	G#	A
C	C	F	G	D	A	Bb
D	D	G	A	E	B	C
E	E	A	B	F#	C#	D
F	F	Bb	C	G	D	Eb
G	G	C	D	A	E	F

This is how you can apply the chart. Suppose you're playing a song in the key of G, but it's a little too high for you to sing, or a little too awkward to play comfortably. Instead of being stuck with it, you have the option of finding a new key. Maybe C suits you better. In that case, just check the chart to find the corresponding I, IV, and V chords for the key of C. Of course, you can do this for any other key as well. Shifting from one key to another is called *transposing*. Now add the following chords to your memory bank so that you'll have a wider selection of keys to transpose into.

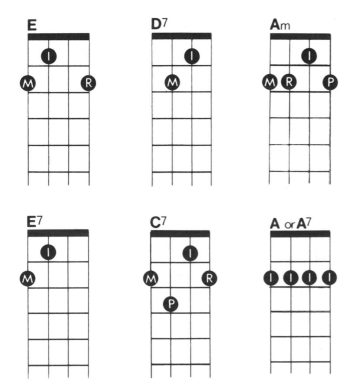

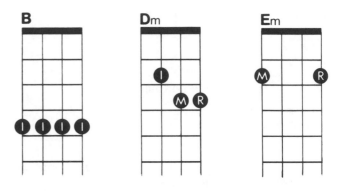

Next, strum through the following two songs and concentrate on making the chord changes as smooth as possible. I'm using the I, IV, and V designations here, so it will be up to you to choose the specific key for each song. Actually, you should play each song in two or three keys to get practice in transposing (heavy lines indicate downbeats; light ones, off-beats).

Red River Valley

```
              I
From this valley they say you are going
 /       /  /     /    /      /     /  /
              I                      V
We will miss your bright eyes and sweet smile;
 /       /  /     /    /      /     /  /   /
              I                  IV
For they say you are taking the sunshine
 /       /  /     /    /      /     /  /
       V                   I
That has brightened our path for awhile.
 /       /    /    /    /    /
```

Come and sit by my side if you love me
Do not hasten to bid me adieu;
But remember the Red River Valley
And the cowboy who loved you so true.

Amazing Grace

```
I                IV        I
Amazing Grace, how sweet the sound
 / /    /    /    /    /  /    /
        I                 V
That saved a wretch like me.
 /    /    /    /    /    /
 I                IV        I
I once was lost but now I'm found
 /    /    /    /    /    /  /    /
        I          V    I
Was blind but now I see.
 /    /    /    /    /
```

If you continue to have trouble changing chords, play the songs more slowly. Take the time to get a clean sound and steady rhythm. That's most important.

Inversions

An inversion is simply another form of the same chord played at a different place on the fingerboard. For instance, you can play a G chord this way:

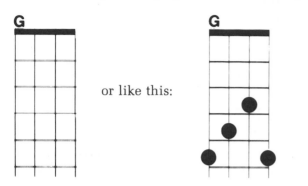

or like this:

Notice that the second inversion has the same fingering as an F chord moved up two frets. To better understand this, you should familiarize yourself with the notes contained in an octave on a piano keyboard. (Again, see Appendix 1 for more details.)

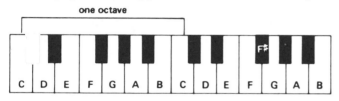

Whenever you go from one piano key to the very next one (black or white), or from one banjo fret to the next consecutive one, you're moving one *half step*. (This half step space is called a chromatic interval.) Thus, there are two half steps between F and G♯ from F to F♯, and from F♯ to G. So if you know an F chord and want to play a G Chord, simply move the position up two frets. To determine the next highest inversion of a G chord, start by fingering a D chord. Since there are five half steps between D and G (refer to the keyboard), just move the D position up 5 frets and you'll find your G.

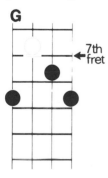

With a little bit of practical application, the concept of inversions will become second nature to you. To help that process along, memorize the arrangement of the notes on the keyboard. It won't take long, and it's knowledge that you'll be able to use not only in dealing with inversions, but also in gaining an overall understanding of the way music works.

Capos

The capo is a handy device which clamps or straps onto the neck of your banjo and allows you to play in different keys without changing basic left hand positions. Since G, C, and D are the positions you'll most often use in a bluegrass context—to give you that driving bluegrass sound—what do you do when you run into someone with an incredibly high voice who insists on singing songs in the key of B♭? Answer: Strap your capo on the third fret and play out of a G position (B♭ is three half steps above G).

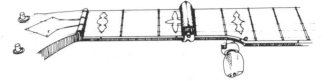

Of course, you'll also have to tune the fifth string up to B♭. This can be accomplished, without fear of breaking the string, by using either railroad tacks or a fifth-string capo (see Appendix 2).

Essentially, the capo makes it easy to transpose from one key to another. This is an instance where the I, IV, V terminology comes in handy. Suppose your band is playing in the key of B and you're capoed at the fourth fret. Since you're playing out of G position, you're thinking in terms of G, C, and D. However, the fiddler and mandolin player aren't using a capo, and are probably looking at things from the perspective of B, E, and F♯. To avoid confusion, all parties involved can refer to these as I, IV, and V chords.

With all this said, let me now play the devil's advocate and suggest to you the possibility of working without a capo. Although the capo gives you total freedom to play in any key, in that very way it can also become a crutch. For instance, you might play for twenty years and never learn your way around the uncapoed key of B; and, in truth, most people don't (I haven't yet). You see, every key has its own particular flavor, determined in large part on the banjo by the relationship of open to fretted strings. Some keys make a lot of use of open strings; others, hardly any. The reason we're so fond of the keys of G, C, and D is that they allow us to play a lot of harmonious open strings, which produce a good, driving, bluegrass sound. We tend to avoid the key of B because the open notes sound discordant (with the exception of the second string, B). This can be pretty discouraging if we just want to sit down and "pick." But if we're willing to spend the time, there's no reason we can't become as comfortable in the key of B as we are in the key of G. I'm not saying it's easy, but it can be done. Don Reno and Bill Keith have already experimented with this idea to varying degrees, and for Pat Cloud it's a way of life. In short, the banjo needs to progress and this can be achieved by expanding our fluency in other keys. If you're a beginner, you shouldn't worry about this right now. For the rest of us, though, it's a task worth undertaking.

Scruggs Style

Now that you have a banjo in your hands, picks on your fingers, and your fingers on the strings, you can start unraveling the mysteries of Scruggs style. This is the one sound that can get you to driving twenty miles over the speed limit in no time at all when it comes over your car radio. It was perfected by Earl Scruggs in the early to mid-1940s, and is still rock solid at the center of every bluegrass banjo player's music, no matter how far out he or she gets.

Rolls

The building blocks of this style are called rolls. A roll refers to the way the right hand plays a series of three or four notes. For instance, there's the forward roll:

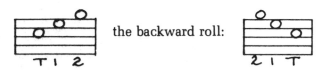

the backward roll:

the forward-backward roll:

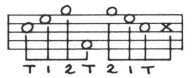

and the T1T2 (or three-finger double-thumbing) roll:

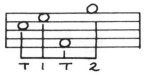

There are, of course, many other right-hand combinations, but you can do quite a lot with just these. Now here's a version of "Nine Pound Hammer," to give you an idea of how these rolls sound when put into context.

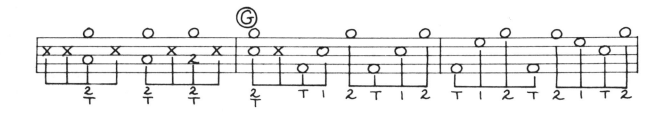

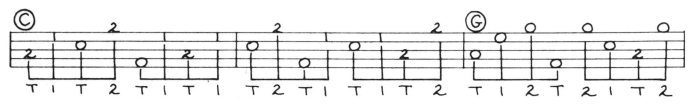

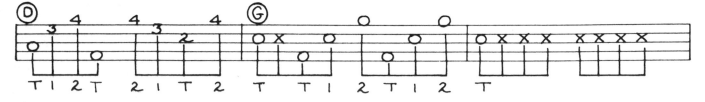

This is just a skeletal version of the tune. So to flesh things out a bit, I'm going to add a few standard Scruggs licks to the recipe.

Licks

In order to play the licks I'm about to show you, you'll need to learn a few simple techniques.

The first is the *slide*. This involves fretting a string on one note and sliding it to another fret on the same string. For example, using the middle finger of your left hand, play these two slides (in tablature a slide is represented by an S).

Now try this. Just as you reach the top of your slide, pick up on the adjacent string with your index finger.

We can take this idea to its logical conclusion by combining the slide with the T1T2 right-hand roll. This gives you two instant Scruggs licks.

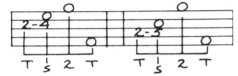

You can also use a forward roll to get these two variations:

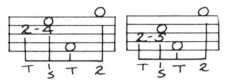

The next technique we're going to examine is the *pull-off*. You can either pull off from one fretted note to another or from a fretted note to an open string. For an example of the former, place the middle finger of your left hand on the third fret of the third string and pull off to your index finger, which should be sitting on the second fret of that same string (in tablature, P = pull-off).

Although you're actually only picking the first note, you should hear the second with almost equal clarity. In a sense, you're plucking the second note with the middle finger of your left hand as you pull it off. In other words, you shouldn't just lift the middle finger straight off the fingerboard, but instead you should push it off in the direction of the ceiling or sky (depending on your environment). In the process, this middle finger may brush against the fourth string, but don't worry about that. When you're actually playing, any extraneous sounds will be camouflaged in the overall flurry of notes. Now to

throw the pull-off into a lick, we can use our old standby, the T1T2 roll.

Remember to pull off just as you're about to pick the second note with your index finger. This will give you two notes for the price of one. To pull off from a fretted note to an open string, try this:

Here's one way of putting this into lick form:

The final technique we're going to deal with right now is the *hammer-on*. Pick the open fourth string and then plop your middle finger down on the second fret.

You've just hammered on. Here, too, we can use either forward or a T1T2 roll to create these licks.

Undoubtedly the most famous hammer-on lick in bluegrass is this next one, which appears in many tunes, including "Foggy Mountain Breakdown":

Now we're going to go back to "Nine Pound Hammer," this time adding some of the licks you've learned, to create a true bluegrass sound. Start off slowly so that every note is crisp and clean, then build up speed. At the same time, concentrate on achieving a smooth, solid rhythm. Even with this relatively simple break, you'll begin to sense some of the real satisfaction that this style has to offer. I've drawn a line over the basic melody notes of the song to give you a more graphic picture of the way Scruggs style works. The melody is all there, but it's integrated with licks and rolls to create a flowing and driving bluegrass sound.

15

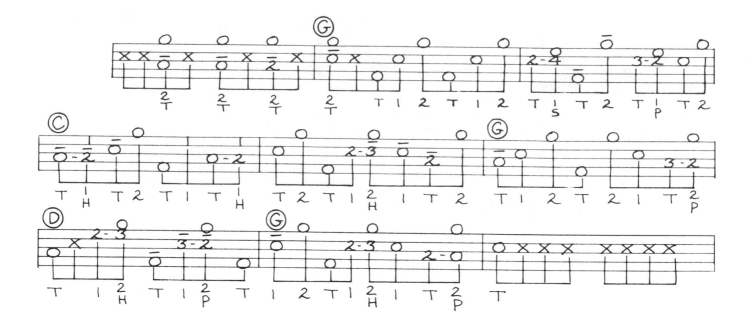

To close off this section, here are a couple of other techniques which don't appear as often as the ones you've already learned, but are nonetheless important.

Choking

Musicians were choking strings long before bluegrass was invented. Some of the older bluesmen, for instance, used chokes to imitate the expressive qualities of the human voice. This added an emotional dimension to their music which couldn't be achieved by the straight fretting of their instruments. Though for the bluesmen, this was undoubtedly an unconscious process, the feelings and techniques weren't lost on Bill Monroe. He put a lot of the blues into his music while he was developing it between the late 1930s and mid-1940s. In fact, Earl Scruggs kicked off his second break on Bill's Bluegrass Breakdown in 1948 by using a bluesy choke lick very similar to this one (an arrow is placed over the notes to be choked):

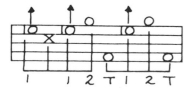

To do this, you should fret the second string with your middle finger and push up until you actually touch the third string.

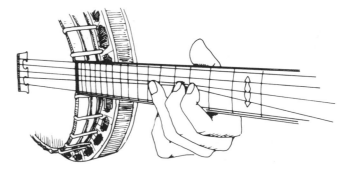

These next two licks are even more strikingly bluesy.

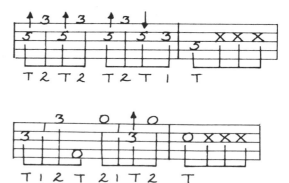

To show you just how far you can take this concept, a friend of mine has worked out some of B. B. King's breaks note for note on the banjo, chokes and all.

Harmonics

Harmonics are the bell-like sounds you'll hear when you touch your strings lightly and directly over certain frets. (This is sometimes known as chiming the strings.) Since the twelfth fret (the half-way point of the string) produces the greatest harmonic resonance of any spot on the banjo, that's precisely where most of the common bluegrass licks utilizing this technique take place.

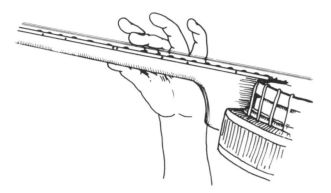

For instance, there's the reveille at the beginning of "Bugle Call Rag" (p. 122):

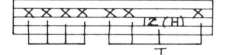

Here, the notes you're getting are an octave above the open strings.

Harmonics can also be found elsewhere on the neck. Since they work on a mathematical basis, they can be found at one-third intervals on the string: at the seventh and nineteenth frets (these will give you a D chord). You can also find them by dividing the string in quarters, so they will be at the fifth fret and just beyond the fingerboard (they both produce a G chord). There are other more obscure harmonics lurking on the fingerboard, such as the B chord harmonic on the ninth fret, but you don't have to worry about them unless you want to.

This next ending lick uses three different harmonic positions:

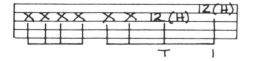

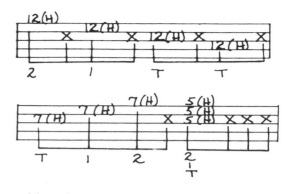

Although it's common to play several harmonics in a row over one fret, you can also mix them up like this:

It's also nice, at times, to sprinkle single harmonics in with your regular notes to add sparkling highlights to your playing. For an example of this, listen to the first minute or so of "Jesse's Girl" from my *Heartlands* album.

Now that you have the basics of Scruggs style under your belt, we can move on to the next development—Reno style.

Reno Style

Don Reno, as you'll find out, later in the book, was working on the three-finger style at about the same time as Scruggs. In the mid-forties, though, he diverged from the mainstream and took a path that opened up new technical vistas on the banjo. The hallmark of this original style was a single string approach that mimicked a flat picking sound by alternating the thumb and index fingers of the right hand. Whereas "Scruggs style" was based to a large extent on chords, this "Reno style" relied primarily on melodic lines. Where before there was no quick, easy way to play a scale on a banjo, it was now a minor technical exercise.
G scale:

We can expand this concept into a full-fledged break with this version of "Nine Pound Hammer."

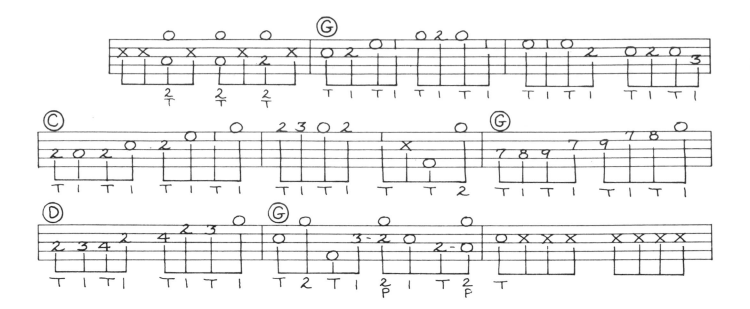

Melodic Style

Although this technique was a tremendous step forward, it didn't provide the full answer. It was still difficult to navigate one's way note for note through a fiddle tune. The left hand positions were often awkward, and the sound was sometimes too choppy to suit the song being played. There had to be an easier route. And there was: the melodic style.

Melodic Style

Melodic style, also known as Keith style, chromatic style, and Yankee banjo playing, (or whatever you wish to call it), was first explored by Bobby Thompson in 1957, while he was playing with Carl Story. A few years later, and several states to the north, Bill Keith was independently developing and popularizing a melodic style of his own. Bill's analytical and creative genius was responsible for setting up an entirely new body of banjo knowledge—licks, tunes, scales, and endings—all based on this fledgling approach.

Today, the melodic style is probably as popular as Scruggs picking, due, in part, to the simplicity of its technique. This is what's involved. Instead of playing two or three successive notes on the same string, find a way to pick the same notes on alternating strings. For instance, in the Reno style you might play this:

In the melodic style it can be done thus:

The trick is to find the easiest, cleanest, and potentially fastest way to pick a melody. To see how this is done, compare this melodic G scale with the one you've already learned in the Reno section.

One of the most important effects of the melodic style has been to put the fifth string on an equal footing with the other four strings. Instead of acting as just a drone, as it does with Scruggs style, it serves as an equal carrier of the melody. Here's a melodic fragment to demonstrate this:

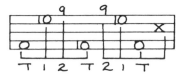

Once you have a basic feel for the inner tickings of this style, play through this melodic version of "Nine Pound Hammer."

Nine Pound Hammer (1)

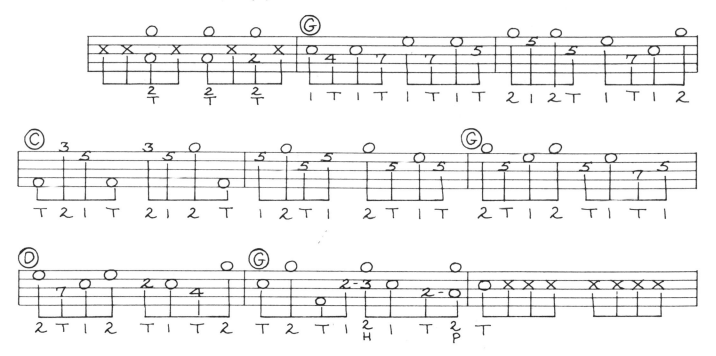

As you can see from the tablature, the melodic style tends to lead you a bit further up the neck so that you can bounce back and forth between open strings and higher, fretted strings. This gives you a smoother sound than, say, the Reno style. But in the process it may lead to a mild case of musical disorientation. For instance, when you want to go from a lower note to a higher one, instead of going up the neck on the same string or going to the next higher string, you often find yourself dropping back to the next lower string. If this feels unnatural to you, don't fret. With time and practice, the melodic style will become as second nature to you as the Scruggs.

Now before going on to the heart of the book, make sure you have a clear understanding of everything you've read so far. If there's a section you skipped over, it may come back to haunt you later. Now's the time for review. Assuming, though, that everything's under control, let's get into it.

The Roots

Bluegrass banjo didn't just mysteriously materialize in the middle of the twentieth century. It took some ninety years of evolution for three-finger picking to culminate in the refined style developed by Earl Scruggs in the 1940s.

As far as I can tell—and these things are somewhat nebulous—it all began with classical banjo back in the 1860s. Eventually this led to the old-time stylings of Charlie Poole, Doc Walsh, Johnny Whisnant, and others who were playing various mutations of the three-finger style in the twenties and thirties. Of these pickers, Snuffy Jenkins seems to have been most responsible for paving the way for Earl Scruggs and Don Reno. Basing his music on a flowing, melody-led style, Snuffy exerted a direct influence on both men, and came about as close as one could to Scruggs style without actually playing it.

In organizing all this information, I gained new insight into the prehistory of bluegrass banjo. I was amazed by the large number of people who were working out of the three-finger style prior to Scruggs. What also surprised me was the remarkable foreshadowing of Earl's playing by two men in particular—Charlie Poole and Frank Jenkins.

I'd like to express my gratitude to Hank Sapoznik for allowing me to tap his considerable knowledge of the material covered in this section, and to Kinney Roorer for providing valuable information on Charlie Poole.

Classic Banjo

The fingerpicking style of banjo was originally a northeastern urban development. It was adapted from parlor-style guitar, which in turn was a spinoff from classical guitar. This parlor style was popularized between the 1850s and 1870s, and was characterized by a light, almost fragile, sound. The technique involved is analagous to the banjo rolls that were undoubtedly based on it.

Classic or fingerpicking banjo developed almost simultaneously (starting in the mid-1860s) with parlor-style guitar. It was, in fact, referred to as the "guitar style," as distinguished from the "banjo style" which described frailing. Frank Converse was apparently the first well-known musician to play banjo in this fingerpicking style. In 1870, he published an instruction book which demonstrated the basic fingerpicking techniques.

It was Henry C. Dobson, however, who was the first banjoist to appear in concert billed as a "classical" performer. This was in the mid-seventies, and Henry's choice of material reflected the tastes of the times: light classical selections, marches, arias, and banjo novelty songs. Dobson and S. S. Stewart,

another banjo manufacturer and classic performer, were responsible for removing the "blackface" minstrel stigma from the banjo. They attempted, instead, to promote it as a legitimate instrument in its own right. In fact, Stewart was somewhat of a fanatic about it; his views appeared in a book he published in 1888 entitled, appropriately enough, "The Banjo." To quote:

> He who can hear, and hear aright; he who possesses what is called a musical ear—he who is by nature capable of perceiving the true grandness and beauties of nature; he who loves to listen to the joyous songs of merry birds, he who sees music and celestial harmony in everything created, is indeed a harmonious and happy individual. He knows there is music in the banjo.

The classic banjo style continued to solidify up to its heyday in the 1880s, when everyone seemed to be playing the instrument, and banjo orchestras were springing up left and right. In 1897, rags were introduced into the banjo repertoire, to add still another dimension to the developing sound. By this time, the classic banjo style had become very ornate and the performer was often required to perform amazing technical gymnastics in order to execute a tune. The attitude was: the more difficult the better.

In reaction to this very serious and highly technical approach, a number of banjoists, including Vester Ossman and Fred Van Eps, looked beyond the standard orchestral pieces for lighter material. Ossman was one of the first classic banjoists to record; and though he was more comfortable on the concert circuit than in the studio, his cylinders were responsible for opening up the repertoire to music written specifically for the banjo.

Van Eps collected a number of the Ossman cylinders and found them a welcome relief from the old-school teachings of his banjo instructor, Alfred A. Farland. Farland wanted Fred to play the heavy classics, including the heaviest of the heavies, Wagner. Van Eps wouldn't hear of it, and instead went on to play fox trots, rags, and novelty tunes—in fact, just about anything he could lay his fingers on. This resulted in a prolific recorded output between 1897, the year he began making cylinders for the Edison Company, and 1926.

The combined influence of Van Eps in the studios (he was one of the world's first studio musicians), and Ossman on the road and on record, helped to spread the gospel of the classic approach. The question is, how did this fingerpicking style make its way south to the likes of Charlie Poole, Frank Jenkins, and the other old-time banjoists? The answer seems to be twofold: via recordings and vaudeville.

Records were a popular source of entertainment

in the South during the early 1900s. It's known for certain that Charlie Poole was listening to Van Eps's recordings. Vaudeville, which was popular from the turn of the century up to the 1930s, also had a hand in spreading the fingerpicking style. Vaudeville shows travelled extensively in the South, and regularly featured classic banjoists. At first, these musicians were imported from the northern urban centers, but as time went on, southern performers, such as Uncle Dave Macon, found their way onto the vaudeville stage.

In addition, there were other, more random, disseminators of the classic style. Fred Bacon, a classic player from the North, toured the South playing local schoolhouses and giving occasional banjo lessons. There were even some native classic players, such as Dana Johnson, who lived in North Carolina.

One thing is certain: the rural southern banjoists didn't learn from instruction books, because very few of them could actually read music. Instead, banjo picking had to be learned through the oral tradition and that's how the three-finger style really spread through the South.

Starting with the strict classic approach, the sound was altered to suit the needs and abilities of the men who practiced it. Some players, like Doc Walsh, retained just the basic roll to accompany their voices. Others, like Frank Jenkins, stayed fairly close to the classic tradition, treating it as the more complex lead style it was originally intended to be.

No matter what form it took, the classic style was directly responsible for the old-time three-finger styles you'll read about in the next section. They, in turn, influenced the modern-day bluegrass banjo sound, which eventually will lead into something else, and on and on. . . .

Frank Jenkins

Frank Jenkins was born in 1888 in Dobson, North Carolina, and died in 1945. Frank was a professional entertainer, and excelled on banjo and fiddle. In fact, he made his living playing at fiddlers' conventions throughout the South. As one story goes, he entered over one hundred fiddle contests, and won a prize at each of them.

During the twenties, Frank was a member of Da Costa Woltz's *Southern Broadcasters*, the band with which he recorded "Home Sweet Home" in 1927. After this, he formed his own group, the *Pilot Mountaineers*, which included Ernest "Pop" Stoneman on guitar.

Stylistically, Jenkins was a master of the three-fingered, classically derived banjo approach, and he had no trouble adapting his playing to that of the older classicists. He differed in this from Charlie Poole, whose technical limitations restricted him to vague approximations of the styles of people like Van Eps. (This isn't to detract from Poole's banjo playing, which glowed in its own light.)

Now, about the following version of "Home Sweet Home": I was amazed the first time I heard it. It sounded as if the same muse who had whispered in Scrugg's ear in the early 1940s had done so for Frank Jenkins in 1927. Jenkins's sound was amazingly close to bluegrass. On closer listening, though, I discovered that he was throwing in two-finger "pinches" to create more of a classic feel. These are bars three and four:

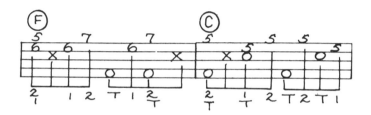

In the final analysis, I think Jenkins's style was halfway between classic & bluegrass. He certainly had roots in the classic tradition. In fact, "Home Sweet Home" was the "Foggy Mountain Breakdown" of the classic style. Also, the finger tremolo that Frank uses in his fifth variation of the tune (not included here) is heavily indebted to Fred Bacon, a banjo manufacturer and respected classic performer. At the same time, Frank's flowing melody lead throughout is astoundingly similar to Scruggs style. I highly recommend that you not only work out this tune, but also pick up a copy of the record on which it appears. It's a real eye opener.

Home Sweet Home

(GCGBD-capo2)
Key of D

Traditional

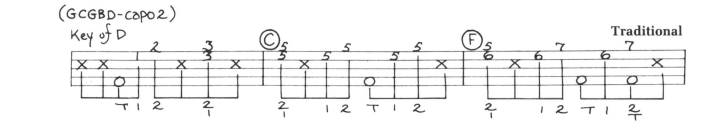

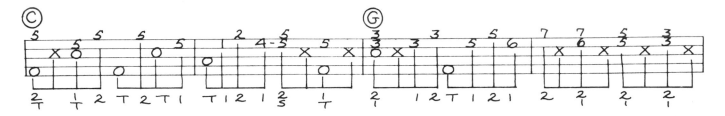

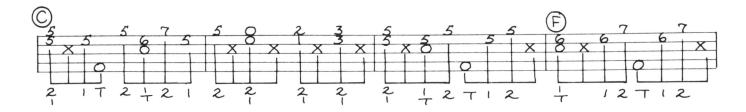

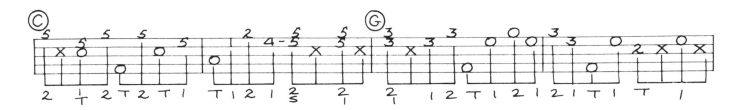

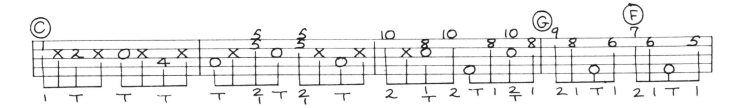

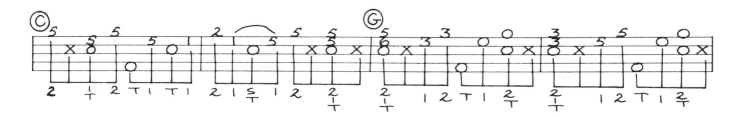

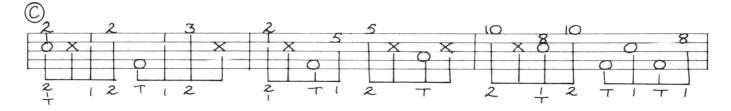

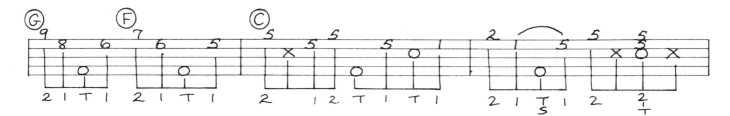

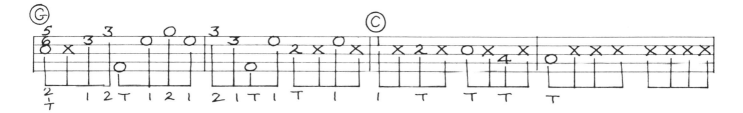

23

Doc Walsh

Aside from being the self-proclaimed "Banjo King of the Carolinas," Doc Walsh was also the father of a unique Hawaiian banjo style that he created by placing pennies under the bridge and using a knife for fretting. This created a "bottleneck banjo" sound which, for some reason, never caught on (with the isolated exceptions of Gus Cannon, Art Rosenbaum, and Blind Eric Flatpick).

Doctor Coble Walsh was born in 1901 in Lewis Fork, North Carolina. He started playing the banjo at the age of four on a fretless instrument made from an old axle-grease box. His first recording—in Atlanta, in 1925—was made in reaction to the so-called Henry Whitter effect. Henry was an old-time guitarist of only average talent who had traveled to New York City in the early 1920s to force himself upon the local recording industry. When Henry's stylings were finally released, other musicians down South felt that they could do as well or better. This was the impetus that got many of them, including Doc, into the studios.

Walsh organized a group—which included Clarence Ashley—called the *Carolina Tarheels*, and began to record prolifically. There's an interesting anecdote that concerns this band. Apparently, Charlie Poole was passing through West Virginia and happened upon a sign advertising a show to be put on by Charlie Poole and the *North Carolina Ramblers*. Curious as to who this might be, Charlie walked into the concert to find Doc Walsh and the *Tarheels* picking merrily away on stage. This blatant act of misrepresentation, however, in no way diminishes Doc's musicianship. Though not a wizard of the strings, he had one of the smoothest three-finger rolls going.

This version of "In the Pines," recorded on April 17, 1926, shows Doc's flowing back-up style to good advantage. As I mentioned before, the traditional role of the banjo in the old-time string bands was that of accompaniment rather than lead. This accounts for the repetitive, forward-backward rolling style that he uses here. It doesn't really go anywhere, but it's perfect in the context of what he's doing. In that sense it's not much different from the simpler back-up techniques of modern bluegrass.

In the Pines

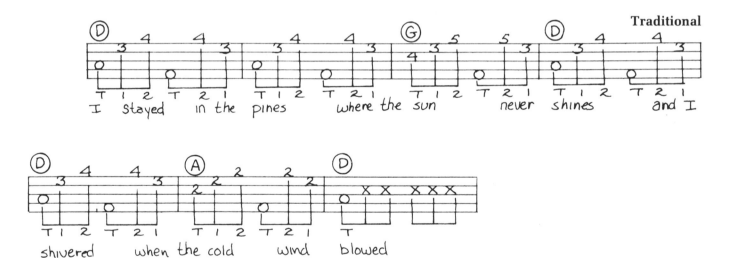

Doc originally sang this in F, but I've transposed into D to avoid capoing. Except for the key change, this is exactly the way he played it back in 1926.

Charlie Poole

Charlie Poole is probably the most well-known of all the old-time three-finger players. His style, like that of Frank Jenkins, is especially noteworthy because it bridged the gaps between classic, old time, and bluegrass banjo.

Charlie was born on March 22, 1892 in Spray, North Carolina, and grew up in impoverished circumstances. In fact, when his father decided to move from one part of the country to another, a wagon was used instead of a truck to carry the family belongings. At age ten, Charlie set out on his own to learn the banjo. He didn't have the benefit of records to listen to because in those days, the only cylinder players available were the coin-operated ones in local theater lobbies. They were a luxury he couldn't afford. In spite of this, his unique banjo style began to take shape. This resulted, in part, from a baseball accident which had left his right hand arched in a permanent picking position.

Charlie's first outside influence was probably Dana Johnson, the classic banjoist mentioned in the preceding section. Johnson, from nearby Greensboro, was no slouch. His considerable talents enabled him to win first prize in the banjo competition at the 1904 St. Louis Exposition. Poole was also

greatly influenced by Fred Van Eps. Charlie must have owned a number of Van Eps recordings, because he rendered old-time versions of Fred's "Sunset March" and "L'Infanta," as well as "Southern Medley," which was a reworking of Van Eps's popular "Dixie Medley." Even so, Charlie generally avoided buying records. However, he did have a number of favorites. He loved the 78s of Blind Blake, a country blues performer. He also did a lot of listening to a Victor recording of "Cherokee Rag" by Big Chief Henry's *Indian String Band*. Just before his death, Charlie even began listening to Broadway show tunes, although he never had a chance to incorporate them into his own music.

In Poole's mind, the banjo's role in the string band was that of a lead instrument playing a strong accompaniment. Expanding on this concept, Poole's was one of the first rural bands to incorporate "breaks" for certain instruments, instead of featuring the usual ensemble playing. This next tab, taken from Charlie's break on "Flop-Eared Mule," is a good example of this phenomenon. It's also remarkable because it represents a transition from his normal, choppy, chordal, three-finger playing, to a more highly evolved, melody-oriented, essentially Scruggsy sound—and this break dates from 1931!

Flop Eared Mule

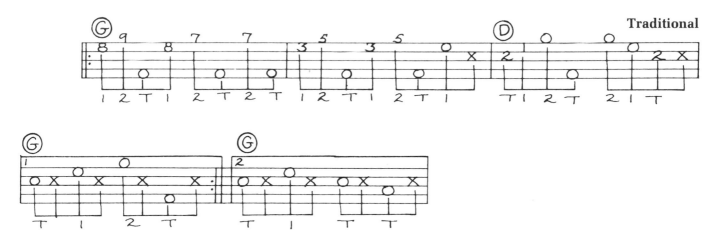

Since this was recorded at Charlie's last session, it's impossible to know where his style would have led. But this was apparently the way he preferred to play. Unfortunately, Columbia Records, and the audiences that crammed into the local schoolhouses to hear Poole, wanted him to stick closer to the familiar old-time style that was his trademark. Still, this "uptown" sound was the direction in which he was

headed at the time of his death.

In the last few weeks of his life, it looked like Charlie's success was assured. He was preparing to go to Hollywood to record a movie soundtrack, and even had his ticket in hand. As fate would have it, though, he became ill and died on May 21, 1931, at his sister's home in Spray.

Johnny Whisnant

Johnny Whisnant was born on December 12, 1921 in Lenoir, North Carolina, in the northwestern tip of the state. Since communications were limited in those days, it meant that he was isolated from the likes of Smith Hammett and Snuffy Jenkins. They were incubating their versions of the three-finger style eighty miles due south in three-finger-rich Cleveland County. So Johnny turned instead to the recordings of Charlie Poole, for inspiration. "I had banjo on my mind as far back as the old Charlie Poole days when he put out that old 'Monkey On A String' bit."*

Although Mozart composed his first symphony at the age of eight, he wasn't that far ahead of Johnny, who had managed to pick up the three-finger roll by the time he was nine. "Anybody who knew me when I was nine years old will tell you the same, that I played with the three-fingered roll exactly similar to the way I play—well, you've heard me play, and I play exactly the way I did then except I've added this bluegrass bit to it since then."

There were two men primarily responsible for this precocious behavior: Mac Crowe and Clay Everheart. Mac was a local entertainer and producer of fiddle conventions who picked with three fingers in a "dobro" style (as Johnny calls it). He would play lead on the first string with his index and middle fingers to create a flatpicking effect, and then alternate his thumb between the third and fifth strings. It was Everheart, however, who really got Johnny started. "He was the first banjo player I ever seen and I've lived a long time and I'd have to say right now that he was the best banjo player that I ever heard in my life." Clay played a choppy forward-backward rolling style. He had recorded for Columbia in the early thirties with the *North Carolina Cooper Boys*.

He was playing with a perfect three-finger roll and I asked him after I had got to the point that I could play it, I said, "Who taught you to play it?" And he called a man's name—it was Hubert Lowe, I believe—and that man taught him the exact roll and I heard an old record that Everheart had, that had a three-fingered roll on it that he said this man who taught him played. It was a little old acetate record, I guess you'd call it. And it had a three-fingered roll on it similar to the one Mr. Everheart used, and that's a long time before Mr. Everheart.

In addition to these stimuli, Johnny was introduced, at age nine, to Carl Story, a fiddler who worked with Johnny's father in the Lenoir furniture factory. On one occasion, the two picked away a lunch hour in a field near the factory. This was the beginning of a working relationship that would last twelve years. From the initial jams and square dances, the two graduated to professional status in 1932 when J. E. Clark, a local entrepreneur, placed

*All quotes courtesy of Ken Irwin and Rounder Records.

them in a band he was forming, *J. E. Clark and the Lonesome Mountaineers*. Though the pay was bad, it was a start. In 1935, the band recorded six sides for Vocalion. They also landed a regular radio show over WSPA in Spartanburg, South Carolina. The sponsor there was Vim Herb, a patent medicine company that produced "Scalf's Indian River Medicine." Evidently, the elixir did nothing for the band's financial woes, and in 1937 Carl and Johnny reorganized the band under the name of *Carl Story and the Rambling Mountaineers*. Johnny stayed with the *Mountaineers* until he was drafted in 1942.

After the war, he was conscripted into the service of the *Lane Brothers*, who were based in Morristown, Tennessee. This was followed by a tour of duty with Willie Brewster, who was working a show out of WIVK, Knoxville, that was hosted by the colorful Cas Walker, a regional department store owner. Since then, Johnny has added his old time bluegrass sound to a number of fine outfits, including the *Bailey Brothers*, Benny and Balley Cain, the *Brewster Brothers*, and Carl Butler.

It's only in recent times that Johnny has gotten some of the recognition he's deserved all along, for being one of the pioneers of the three-finger style. With his panoramic overview of the development of bluegrass banjo, Johnny's insights and opinions are especially valuable. These are some of them.

Now that three-fingered thing comes up in every conversation anybody has. I won't begin to say where it started 'cause I don't know. But I believe it goes back to the first people who ever played a banjo, 'cause I imagine they tried with two fingers and then a thumb and then tried to add the other one on. I imagine it went back as far as trying to play with all four fingers, but this finally wound up being the best thing. But I tell you where this thing, in my opinion, gets crossed up. Now in talking about a three-fingered roll, you're going back to two people and that's Snuffy Jenkins and Earl Scruggs. Now both of those men have come up with a thing of their own that they were the inventors of. Earl came up with his type of thing that he did and it was his. But then the difference is not in the right hand. See, a three-fingered roll can be adapted in several different ways, with down playing from a chord—just a chord. And every time you set your fingers down, you play from a chord and still play a three-fingered roll. But then you take Earl's type of thing, where it differs from the way I started playing the banjo. Where the banjo playing differs is instead of playing from a chord, like I did, and like I started playing and like I still think is the best way in the world to play a banjo because you've got more value to it. Now where I think that differs from Earl, he started doing his in open strings, doing most of his picking in a G position. Now that's where it differs but not in the right hand. The right hand is the roll. You see, a three-finger roll can be varied in a hundred different ways and you're still playing with three fingers. But you can't condemn a man if he starts something on his own. Now, like Reno—when he first started playing the banjo I thought he was the greatest thing since Lindbergh, but he didn't play a five-string banjo when he first started. When he first started playing the banjo, which I thought was great now, he played a four-string banjo and didn't use the fifth. Now you listen to "Using My Bible For a Roadmap," which is the most distinct thing you've ever seen. The only time he hits the fifth string is not while he's playing his melody, it's when he's backing up. You know he sings a line and you can hear him tip that fifth string. But that's also a three-fingered roll. He also had him a three-finger roll, but he didn't use the fifth string like I do in my way of playing and like Earl does in his. So the variation of where people get the origin arguments out—they say Earl Scruggs started three-fingered roll. Now we're talking about youngsters that was beginning to listen to banjo playing about the time Earl broke out. They think of Earl because that's all they heard. They didn't hear anything beyond. I mean, I thought it was good when I come out of the army. But it took some getting used to after what I had been playing for years and still do. I play Earl's stuff because I like it, but it was a thing that was his and it belonged to him. So that's where the difference is in this three-finger roll business. Now I think you'll agree that it's been done from the time the first man picked up a banjo. He was experimenting trying to play all of them and I imagine a few tried to play with their toes even. I know Emory Martin use to take his shoe off and play with his toe 'cause if you make up your mind you're going to play a damn banjo, you're going to play that thing one way or the other.

Style

As Johnny mentioned, he prefers a chordal approach to his music. Note the following example, taken from his playing with Carl Story in 1939:

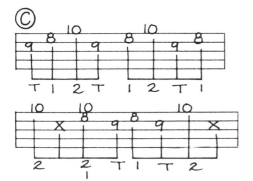

He stays right on top of that C chord and then applies the same basic roll to the other static chord positions. As you can see, though, it isn't a completely flowing roll. The second bar is interrupted by a sixteenth-note rest and a pinch, both of which tend to tie it back to the styles of the late twenties and early thirties. Compare it, for instance, with Charlie Poole's turn-around on "Bill Mason":

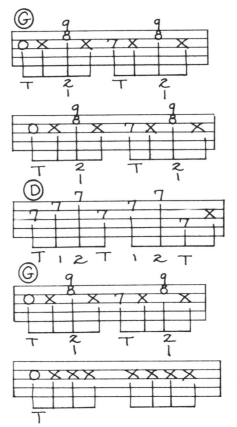

Notice the similar reliance on chord positions (ninth fret G and seventh fret D), and the parallel intertwining of pinches and forward rolls. Side by side, these examples demonstrate an obvious stylistic link between the two men.

Johnny's version of "Maple Leaf Rag" represents a mixture of old-time and modern approaches to a standard classical piece. *Part A* is more closely related to Johnny's style of the thirties—a bit on the choppy side, and played almost exclusively out of chordal positions. *Part B*, on the other hand, is basic bluegrass. It has more of a flow, and includes several common Scruggs licks, elements that were added to Johnny's playing sometime after the mid-forties.

The right-hand patterns in both sections are generally restricted to forward and backward rolls, which further indicates the old-time influence. I should mention, though, that "Maple Leaf Rag" does not reveal the full scope of Johnny's playing. On other tunes, such as "Claim Jumper," from his first Rounder record, he picks a fully developed Scruggs style, and even allows a couple of melodic licks to creep in here and there. This puts Johnny in a unique position. Whereas most players of his era developed their own styles and stuck to them, Johnny was flexible enough to root himself in the more rugged old-time sound while absorbing the latest developments in banjo technique. In a sense, he has become a walking history of three-finger playing, and for this reason his music deserves to become more widely known.

Maple Leaf Rag

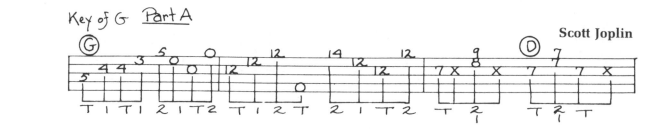

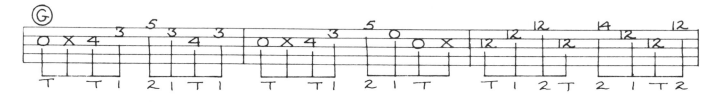

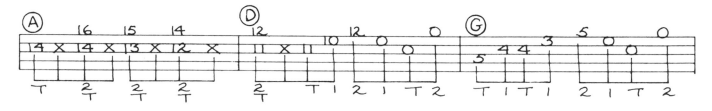

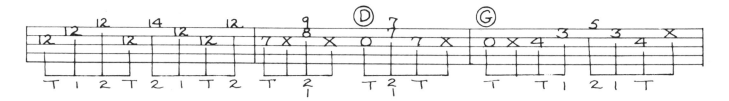

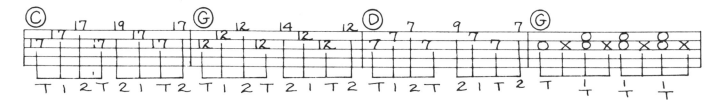

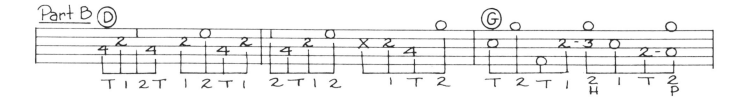

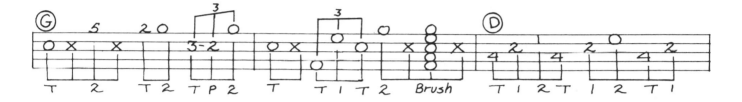

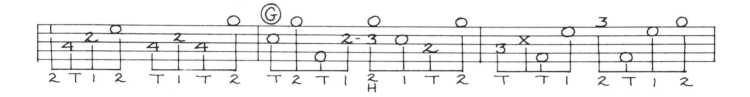

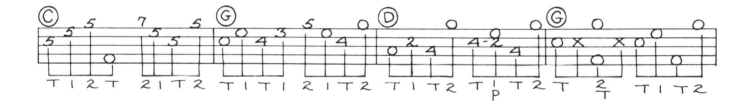

Snuffy Jenkins

There was other fellas that played with three fingers before Snuffy, but he was the first one who ever put it together. It's like seeing a river winding and you don't know where it's going and then finally you see it straightened out going into the ocean; that's the best way I can explain it. When I heard Snuffy, I could see that he had unwound something and straightened it out to the point where it did have a flowing melody to it and not a bunch of jerks and stops and this, that, and the other thing. He had perfected, as far as I'm concerned, a three-finger roll.

—Don Reno

Dewitt "Snuffy" Jenkins was born October 27, 1908, in Harris, North Carolina. As a child, Snuffy was surrounded by music. He grew up to be what you might call the grandaddy of modern-day three-finger picking.

There was seven of us in the family and, of course, just about all of them played a little bit, not much professionally, but me and my brother Virl, we played more together than anybody, and he was a fiddler and I was playing the banjo. We had a band of our own and we were playing for dances and fiddler's conventions around in the twenties.

In 1927 we started playing with two fellas who both played a three-finger style of banjo. One was Rex Brooks, and one was Smith Hammett and they both lived in Cleveland County, North Carolina, right around where Earl Scruggs was born and raised. So I heard those fellas playing and that kind of stuck with me a little bit, and I picked it up from them. [It's interesting to note that Smith Hammett was also a prime influence on Earl Scruggs.] Rex, he was working at the telephone company, and he played with his fingernails and the thumbpick which made it a good clear sound, but it wasn't too loud, you know. And Smith Hammett, I believe he was a farmer. He said he played with his fingernails 'til his middle finger got so sore from playing for dancing he couldn't stand it and he went to using his index and ring fingers with picks. He was a good banjo player, Smith—he was a good dancer too—light on his feet, you know—cloggin'. He was really a card. A little short guy. He had sort of a drinking problem too. Well, all of them would take a drink, but I understand he was pretty mean when he got to drinking.

Unfortunately, Smith never recorded, but he left his mark on both Snuffy and Earl.

When he was nineteen, Snuffy began working professionally and by the time he was twenty-six was playing on the popular Crazy Water Barn Dance out of Charlotte, North Carolina. In 1936, he became one of *J. E. Mainer's Mountaineers*, replacing Wade Mainer on banjo. The following year, the band moved from North Carolina to Columbia, South Carolina and radio station WIS. There they teamed up with announcer Byron Parker, the Old Hired Hand. Snuffy describes what it was like travelling around with that band in the late thirties. "We didn't even have a P. A. system. We'd play a lot of these little old rabbit school houses down there. Wouldn't hold over a couple of hundred, you know; fifteen and twenty-five cents, and five of us made a living like that. No electricity." After J. E. Mainer left, the group became known as *Byron Parker's Mountaineers*, and later as the *Hired Hands*. In 1939, fiddler Homer "Pappy" Sherrill joined the band and formed a musical alliance with Snuffy which lasts to this day.

It was during the late thirties and early forties that Don Reno and Earl Scruggs began coming around (independently of each other) to learn from Snuffy. Although Snuffy is often credited with teaching them both to play, he's more modest about his contribution. "I don't claim to have taught Earl or Don, either one, anything. They'd come around to where we was playing in a show date, and naturally I'd show them whatever I could if they wanted me to. Don Reno claims that I taught him everything he knows 'cause he was playing in South Carolina too."

In the years that followed, Snuffy continued to play on WIS radio and television. But ultimately he found it in his best interest to leave. "I quit on account of my health. I was starving to death." So today Snuffy is working for a Chevrolet dealership in Columbia, South Carolina, occasionally stealing away with Pappy to play clubs, festivals, and even a ballet here and there. I should add that in addition to being a fine banjo player, Snuffy is also a crackerjack guitarist, washboard player, and comedian.

Style

Because Snuffy played such an important role in the early development of bluegrass banjo, I've included "Up Jumped the Devil," recorded in 1940 with *Byron Parker's Mountaineers*. This will give you some idea of what his disciples, Reno and Scruggs, were listening to back then. I should mention that this is not a complete break. Recording techniques being what they were in 1940, solos were sometimes drowned out by the accompanying instruments, or, as in this case, by the spirited shouting of one of the band members. Here, we've lost the end of Snuffy's break. But the remainder is intact, and reveals a syncopated forward-rolling approach that fluidly integrates melody and three-finger style. In fact, Snuffy follows Pappy Sherrill's fiddle lines note for note. This marks a technical advance over such players as Charlie Poole and Doc Walsh, who, for the most part, entrenched themselves in more limited chordal patterns. It could be said that Frank Jenkins beat Snuffy to the punch with his 1927 recording of "Home Sweet Home." In truth, Frank had incorporated the melody in his classically oriented

finger style. However, the overall flow was interrupted by numerous two-finger pinches and rests. Snuffy, on the other hand, was able to maintain an unimpeded right-hand flow and combine it with the melody to produce a new sound that was one step away from Scruggs style.

"Nancy Rowland," recorded thirty-one years later, is an example of Snuffy's playing today. You can see that his approach hasn't changed markedly in that time. He still favors the syncopated sound produced by forward rolls stacked back to back. In fact, when I spoke with him, he said that he was playing "Nancy Rowland" the same way in the 1930s. This is very interesting because if you'll look at the third bar of *Part B*, you'll notice a subtle melodic lick peeking out from a forward roll:

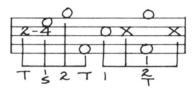

Though this is only a tidbit, it's intriguing to think that Snuffy was delving into melodics when Bill Keith and Bobby Thompson were still in diapers.

Of further interest is the first measure of *Part B*, which features this common bluegrass slide:

If Snuffy was playing like this back in the late thirties, it would make his contribution to bluegrass banjo very direct indeed. It would mean that Scruggs licks were not Scruggs licks, but rather Jenkins licks. Again, the question of who taught what to whom in the late thirties and early forties, is hazy at best. But it's safe to say that Snuffy Jenkins laid down a great deal of basic groundwork for the bluegrass styles that followed.

Up Jumped the Devil

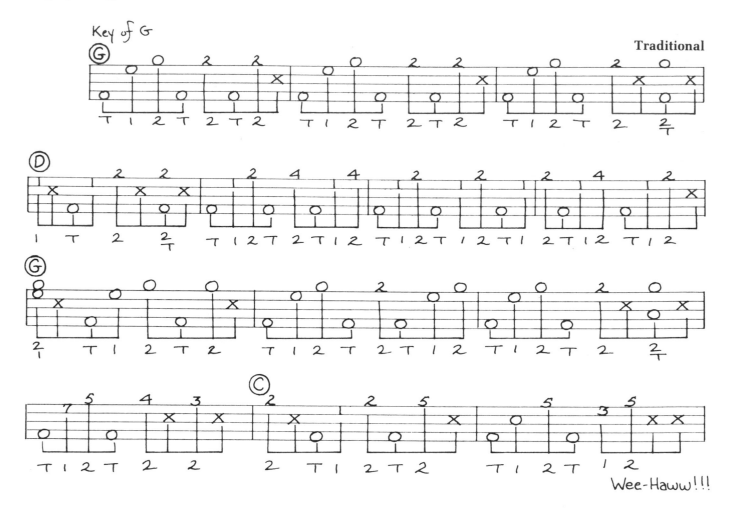

Wee-Haww!!!

Nancy Rowland

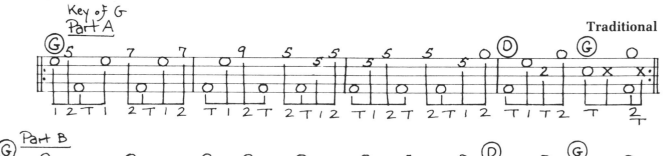

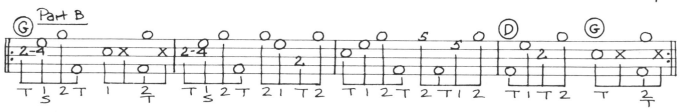

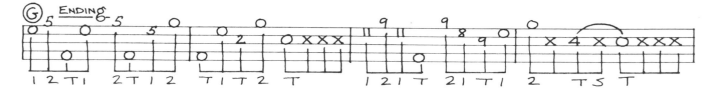

The Mainstream

I'll start this section by admitting that mainstream is a somewhat misleading title. It doesn't really take into account Bill Keith's forays into jazz or Sonny Osborne's occasional flirtations with the bluegrass avant garde. At the same time, I think it's the best way to package the pickers who have helped to create, strengthen, and at times stretch, the standard banjo vocabulary we use today.

Initially, most of these players were adding something new to the sound of bluegrass banjo. Earl Scruggs, of course, started things rolling in 1945; Don Reno put in his own variations soon after that; and Bill Keith went even farther afield in 1963. Yet today all three are considered part of the bluegrass establishment. This doesn't mean they should be totally confined to that category—that's a sure way to limit creativity. Earl Scruggs, for instance, played straight bluegrass for twenty-three years, and then placed himself in a rock band. Allen Shelton worked with Jim and Jesse for six years, and then had a hankering to record with the Nashville Symphony. People have to grow, and no one label can contain that growth. Still, all of the musicians included in this section flow with the mainstream in this sense: the majority of us pattern our playing after theirs.

Earl Scruggs*

Unless you somehow managed to miss hearing the theme from "The Beverly Hillbillies" or *Bonnie and Clyde*, you won't need any introduction to Earl Scruggs.

Earl is, of course, the recognized father of modern bluegrass banjo playing. There are very few, if any, pickers playing today who have not been influenced by him. He was born into a banjo-playing family on January 6, 1924, in Flint Hill, North Carolina. His father, George; older brothers, Junie and Horace; and older sisters, Eula Mae and Ruby, all played. From the ages of four to eight, Scruggs played with a two-finger style.

> *My older brother Junie, and a fellow who's been long dead, name of Smith Hammett, Mac Woolbright, a lot of several banjo pickers in North Carolina played what we now call three-finger banjo pickin'. Actually it's two fingers and the thumb; but I played the older style, I mean by that only with one finger. But it was my ambition to play like Smith Hammett or these other people, and I came up with the style I'm hooked with, you might say.***

Earl's breakthrough came when he was fourteen. He had been playing almost unconsciously with three fingers instead of two. Suddenly, he realized what he was doing.

> *I found that the melody line had been smoothed out, had become less jerky and flowed easily from one note to the next in a continuous regular pattern, rather than jumping and jerking along. What had happened was that I was playing in fiddle patterns rather than in banjo ones.*
>
> *I kept playing one piece for a whole week— that was "Reuben"—until I got that flowing and unbroken pattern I wanted. Then I played it for my brother Junie when he came home. He wasn't too impressed, to tell the truth, and told me that others had been playing that way for years. And there had been several others. He was right there.*
>
> *There were several people right in my area, in fact, who were playing in a three-finger style. There was Smith Hammett, an older man, who used three fingers, but whose approach was still pretty much in the old way. Then there was Fischer Hindley, who used to broadcast with his Aristocratic Pigs group. He used three fingers instead of two, and so did Snuffy Jenkins, another local banjoist. But all of these styles were based in the old, ragged, heavily syncopated method. I learned something from*

*Except where otherwise indicated, the quotes in this section are from "Earl Scruggs, and the Sound of Bluegrass," by Pete Welding in Sing Out, April–May 1962, pp. 4–7.

**Bluegrass Unlimited, July 1967, p. 2.

the playing of each of these men, but none of them had what I wanted. So I had to develop it on my own.

It took a long time, but finally I got to the point where I was playing what was in my mind. It got so I could play just about any tune in the three-finger method, and in any key, too. That was another thing I worked out—the use of capos for key changes. Up until then, just about everything was played in three keys—G. C. or D. But now, with the use of capos, I could play in any key with complete freedom.

By the time he was fifteen, Scruggs was playing his own version of the three-finger style with the *Carolina Wildcats* on the Gastonia radio station, some thirty miles from Flint Hill. In 1939 he went to WSPA radio in Spartanburg, South Carolina with the *Morris Brothers*, the group responsible for bringing "Salty Dog" into the country repertoire. In the early years of World War II, Scruggs temporarily set aside his music for a factory job.

In December 1945, Earl joined Bill Monroe's group. The move changed his life, and also ultimately defined the banjo's role in a bluegrass band. Monroe's appearances in the Grand Ole Opry and on the road, gave Earl a chance to showcase his style throughout the South. Bill describes how Earl came to work for him.

Earl Scruggs needed a job. I had three appointments with him, and I missed the first two ones, and the third one I went down to where he was at, and Howdy Forrester was the man who got Earl Scruggs the job with me. So when I heard Earl, I knew that that banjo picking would fit my music. It all came from a man in North Carolina named Snuffy Jenkins. That's where Earl learned from, and all the pickers that played three-finger style. But he could help take lead breaks like the fiddle and would be a great help to me. So that's why the banjo was in my music. *

Lester Flatt was playing guitar with Monroe when Scruggs joined. and in March 1948, Lester and Earl left to start their own group, the *Foggy Mountain Boys*. The 1950s saw this band blossom into one of the tightest units in bluegrass history. Earl's flawless banjo playing and Lester's sweet singing—supported by a host of top-notch sidemen including Mac Wiseman, Benny Martin, Josh Graves, Curly Sechler, and Paul Warren—combined to turn out one classic recording after another. They recorded first for Mercury, and then for Columbia. Although initially their popularity was limited to the South, the folk boom of the early sixties changed that. Lester and Earl found themselves playing at the Newport Folk Festival and Carnegie Hall. Suddenly a lot of northern urbanites were slowing down "Flint Hill Special" to figure out Earl's licks note for note. By the late sixties, Flatt and Scruggs were probably the most popular bluegrass performers in the country. But personal tensions had begun to surface; so in 1969, Lester and Earl went their separate ways. Soon afterwards, the *Earl Scruggs Revue* was formed by Earl and his sons, Randy and Gary. Even though the banjo sound remained the same, the bluegrass format was altered to include electric instruments, drums, and, on occasion, piano.

I stayed in bluegrass too long. I felt I had gone as far as I could go with the type of music I was playing a few years ago. I wanted to make progress with my music, and I think that's what I've done. I try to keep an open mind. I realize time won't stand still and wait for the old dress codes and the old haircuts, and the old songs to come back around. *

Style

Up to this point, I've concentrated on the surprisingly large number of people who played in a bluegrass-like, three-finger style before Scruggs did. I say bluegrass-like because, as far as I can tell, no one made full use of the standard licks which came to typify bluegrass until Earl appeared on the scene in the mid-1940s. He was really the first to perfect the three-finger, North Carolina-style of picking. I'm aware that this is a dangerous statement to make because Don Reno claims to have been playing in a style very similar to Scruggs in the early to mid-forties. As far as I know, no examples of Don's music were recorded at this time, so it is impossible to determine how close to Scruggs his style really was. However, if the two were playing in essentially the same way, they probably arrived there independently. Suffice it to say that Earl put the banjo back on the map (with unequaled timing and finesse.)

The following version of "Molly and Tenbrooks," recorded with Bill Monroe on October 28, 1947, is an excellent example of the way Earl transformed the older three-finger styles. Notice that he makes liberal use of the forward roll—also commonly employed by Snuffy and Charlie Poole—to produce a hard-driving sound. However, he has added his soon-to-become-standard Scruggs licks throughout, as a means of carrying the melody. This element, perhaps more than any other, made Monroe's group of the mid-to-late forties the prototype for all future bluegrass bands. Notice, especially, the lick in the second measure which became the "hook" for "Foggy Mountain Breakdown" several years later. In addition, the bars that follow are peppered with the pull-offs, hammer-ons, and slides which constitute the basic fabric of Scruggs style as we know it today.

Turning to the right hand, Earl favored a thumb lead in order to really punch out the melody. This isn't as apparent in the first two-thirds of the tune because the melody occurs on the higher strings. However, it becomes obvious in the last third, where the melody is exclusively thumb led.

Old Time Music, Spring 1975.

Atlanta Constitution July 26, 1974, p. 7.

Taken together, these characteristics indicate that Earl single-handedly standardized a new way of playing the banjo. Though rooted in the past, the sound was smoother than the older three-finger styles. With the addition of the all-important Scruggs licks, it became the perfect complement for the excitingly explosive drive of Monroe's mandolin. In fact, by 1947, Earl had perfected his style to such an extent that there has since been no need to improve on his formula. His "Molly and Tenbrooks" sounds as contemporary now as it did when it was first recorded—and that's a testament to Earl's remarkable creativity.

Molly and Tenbrooks

(Ten-Brooks and Molly)

Bill Monroe

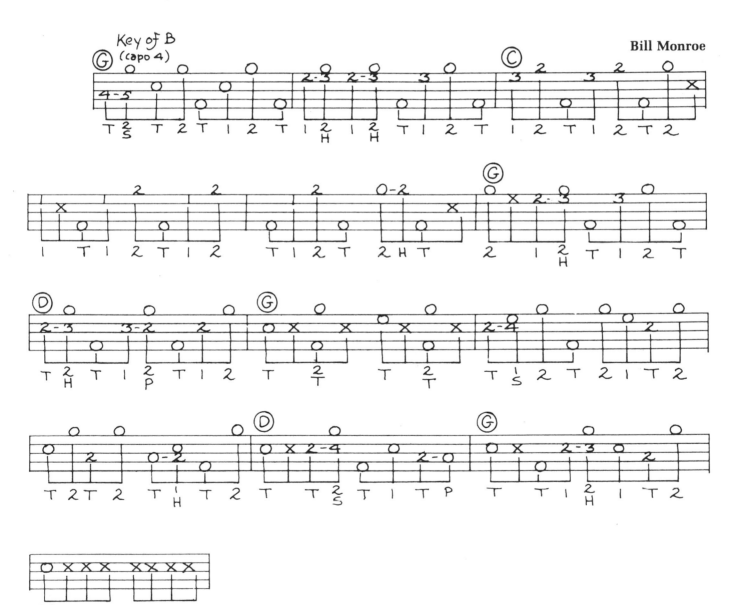

Don Reno

Although Earl Scruggs is universally heralded as the father of bluegrass banjo, if it hadn't been for World War II, we might all be playing "Reno style" today. It seems that in the fall of 1943, Bill Monroe brought his traveling tent show to Spartanburg, South Carolina; Don's home town. After the show, Don and the *Bluegrass Boys* got into a jam session in a local hotel room, and Monroe apparently thought enough of Reno's playing to offer him a job. "I told him I would go volunteer in the army. If they didn't take me I'd agree to work with him. But they took me. In the meantime, Scruggs was turned down for some reason or another and he went to work with Bill, I guess in '45." Since both Don and Earl were playing similar styles, it may have been lucky timing that gave the glory to Earl. But to backtrack a little. . . .

Don was born February 21, 1927. By the time he was five, he realized he had a natural affinity for the banjo.

*My brother had a band when I was a little boy and they would gather at his house and rehearse. That was back when bands rehearsed. And they'd go to eat supper, kept watching their instruments and I was afraid to touch them. So one time I finally did get up enough courage to pick up Leonard Snyder's banjo, and it amazed me just about as much as any-*thing I ever had to amaze, because in a very few seconds I was picking out "May I Sleep in Your Barn Tonight Mister."*

From this auspicious beginning, Don began working on the popular two-finger style of those days.

In 1938, though, he met Snuffy Jenkins, and by the next year he was picking with three fingers.

I caught Snuffy at different schoolhouses and told him I was learning to play. He became very interested in me, much to my surprise, and told me to put the third pick on. If it felt good, it felt rotten, regardless of how much aggravation it caused, to keep using it because it would eventually turn into a pattern that I could use the third finger. The way he started me on was like you number your thumb one, then the two fingers two and three. You know—1, 2, 3/1, 2, 3/1, 2, 3. In other words to keep your roll flowing. He favored the forward roll, I'd say. Back when I first heard him, he played "Cumberland Gap," "Sally Goodin," and "Dear Old Dixie." [This is interesting because Earl recorded "Dear Old Dixie" in the fifties and takes credit for its composition.] He took credit for it, but I heard Snuffy Jenkins play "Dear Old Dixie" when me and Scruggs was little boys. Earl's never given Snuffy credit, which irks me very much in one sense because Smith Hammett didn't have his stuff together. He gives Hammett credit for . . . well, a horse gallop on the banjo. There's not very much technique in that. But Jenkins played "Cumberland Gap" just as clean in the early thirties as me and Scruggs played it after we became known banjo players. North Carolina and South Carolina was the only two states Snuffy ever worked in, so naturally he didn't get the world-wide acclaim that me and Scruggs got. Now it may sound to you that I'm bitter towards Scruggs, but I'm not. He's always been a good friend of mine. I've always thought highly of him.

Apparently, Don had actually run into Scruggs by the early 1940s, and even feels that Earl may have been influenced by him to some extent.

I knew Earl. Earl started after I had started playing professionally. He used to come over to the studio in Spartanburg where I was working and he'd watch our radio show. Finally, Earl told me that he played banjo. We were both teenage boys at the time. Earl was very backwards back then. That was about 1942. This was when Snuffy had sold me an old Mastertone Gibson, and Earl kept trying to trade me out of the Gibson with a Sears and Roebuck banjo that he had. I knew that banjo he was playing was something I didn't want. In 1948 I finally traded with him and he got a hold of it.

Don's first professional experience came in 1940, when he was twelve. He joined the Morris Brothers, Wiley and Zeke. They were foreshadowing the standard bluegrass instrumentation by sporting guitar, mandolin, fiddle, banjo, and bass (it wasn't until about two years later that Bill Monroe added a banjo to the *Bluegrass Boys*). While Don was still with the *Morris Brothers*, he received an offer to play with Arthur Smith. He accepted it, and Earl took his place with Wiley and Zeke.

In late 1943, Don enlisted in the army. He spent part of his time in the horse cavalry at Fort Riley, Kansas, and the rest in more exotic locales, like Burma and Bombay. When he got back home, he found that Earl was working for Monroe.

> *As far as him beating me to the front, I never did care about that. I think he did me a favor. He caused me to change my style. When I come back from the army, why everybody said "You play like Earl Scruggs." So I started a style of my own—single string style, double notes, slow stuff. Nobody played slow stuff on the banjo back then or a double roll. I knew the neck of a flat top like the back of my hand; and the second, third, and fourth strings of a banjo and guitar are the same and the first string is two pitches flat from a guitar string, so you can figure it out from there. I changed my style because I wanted to update the banjo. At this time, it seemed the banjo was more popular in the South, and I wanted to get it across the Mason-Dixon line. I figured to do this you'd have to play stuff besides "Old Joe Clark" and "Sally Goodin."*

This idea led Don to the pop tunes of the twenties, thirties, and forties. "I listened to everybody—Glenn Miller was a favorite of mine, Guy Lombardo, all of them; Benny Goodman, the western outfits—Bob Wills, *Sons of the Pioneers*, anybody who was on record or who I could hear on the radio. When I heard a new sound or a new lick I tried to absorb it and place it."

In the spring of 1948, Don finally got his chance to play with Monroe. Although this was a good opportunity, it meant putting his own style on the shelf in favor of the more traditional three-finger style that Bill's music required.

> *I tuned in the Opry one Saturday night, didn't hear Earl and figured he was gone. So I took off for Nashville, and Bill had pulled out for Taylorsville, North Carolina, and I caught him there on a Monday night. Earl wasn't with him and I actually came backstage and tuned my banjo up and got on the stage and started playing with him because I knew he was hunting for a banjo player in that style and I knew there was very few of them to be had. The only ones I knew of at that particular time was Snuffy, Hoke [Jenkins—Snuffy's nephew], Earl, and myself. So I went to work for Bill and played the stuff that he was wanting to hear, old turkey to me.*

Don stayed with Monroe about two years. Then returned to Greenville, South Carolina. There he or-

ganized the *Tennessee Cutups*, the band that he fronts, to this day. The *Cutups* shifted around for a couple of years. First they moved to Roanoke; then to Wheeling, West Virginia; and finally back to South Carolina. There, Don took on tall and lanky Red Smiley as his partner in 1951.

> *We were on the side of the unknown, so to speak, at that time, and that's very poor country to go to and try to organize a band anyway. The people are not there and the money's not there either. So we disorganized in the spring of '52 after recording sixteen sides for King; and the first release came out, I think, about sixteen weeks after we disbanded. If we'd stuck it out about six more weeks we'd 'a been alright. "I'm Using My Bible For A Roadmap," you know, was one of our biggest records.* *

This case of bad timing prompted Don to go back with Arthur Smith, who was operating out of Charlotte, North Carolina. In 1955, the two used tenor and five-string banjo to record the original version of "Feudin' Banjos." This is the tune that eventually spawned Eric Weissberg and Steve Mandell's "Theme From Deliverance," and the resultant tangle of legal feuding. That same year, the demand for Reno and Smiley intensified as a result of their King recordings. They decided to reunite. This new version of the *Cutups*—based first out of Richmond, and then out of Roanoke—featured John Palmer (from the original group), and Mack Magaha on fiddle. In addition to being one of the classic bluegrass bands of all time, they were prolific in their output of new tunes (many of them penned by Reno). They even managed to get a few songs on the country charts, a rare feat for a bluegrass group. Don and Red finally parted company in February 1965, as a result of Red's frail health. Bill Harrell, who had played mandolin for the *Cutups* in 1956, moved into the guitar spot. Although Red returned for a short period before his death in January 1972, Bill stayed on. Today, with Ed Ferris on bass and Buck Ryan on fiddle, Don and the *Cutups* are still going strong.

Style

Although Don Reno is considered to be a traditional bluegrasser, his playing often comes from the "outside." His banjo style—eternally surprising and eclectic—combines single string flashes; double-time flurries; fast, jazzy full-chord passages; and unexpected right-hand permutations: sometimes all of this takes place in the space of one song. Considering this wealth of original music, it's surprising that more people haven't gotten up off their fingerpicks to figure some of it out. Oh, almost everybody uses the single string technique to one degree or another; but beyond that, very few have attempted to really explore the intricacies of his style. So in the following paragraphs, I'm going to do just that.

Bluegrass Unlimited, November 1967, p. 5.

"Mama Don't Allow" is an example of the composite approach mentioned above. It starts with two bars of Don's own single string picking, which, incidentally, turns out to be a musical quote from the tune "Silver Bell." (You may want to excerpt this lick for your own playing.)

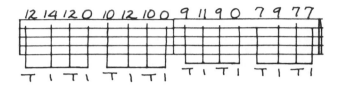

From here, the tune moves into an old-time-sounding chordal lick (in the third bar), followed by more old-time open forward rolling (in the fourth measure). This leads into two bars of straight-ahead bluegrass. Then it reverts to four more bars of fixed chordal playing in the old-time vein. For the ending, Don chooses a bluegrassy left-hand position, but throws in strictly Renoesque right-hand rolls. This personalized approach also crops up in "When You and I Were Young, Maggie." Check the second measure of that tune:

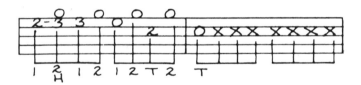

Here's a more Scruggsified way to play the same melody:

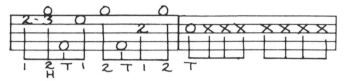

These original twists that Don puts into standard licks lead me to believe that he had come up with his own fully developed three-finger style—including licks—prior to, or simultaneously with, Scruggs. I have some resistance to saying this because we've always considered Earl to be the single-handed inventor of bluegrass banjo. But from what Don has said, and from what I saw when I examined his style, I have a feeling he was right there on the edge with Scruggs in the early forties.

There's one more thing you should listen for in Don's tunes: catchy licks. His music is full of them. Usually, they can be transplanted to good advantage in to your own playing. Try this lick from the second C chord in "Maggie":

Remember, Don has a lot to offer. So when you tire of all those ascending and descending melodic runs, you should give him a try.

Mama Don't Allow

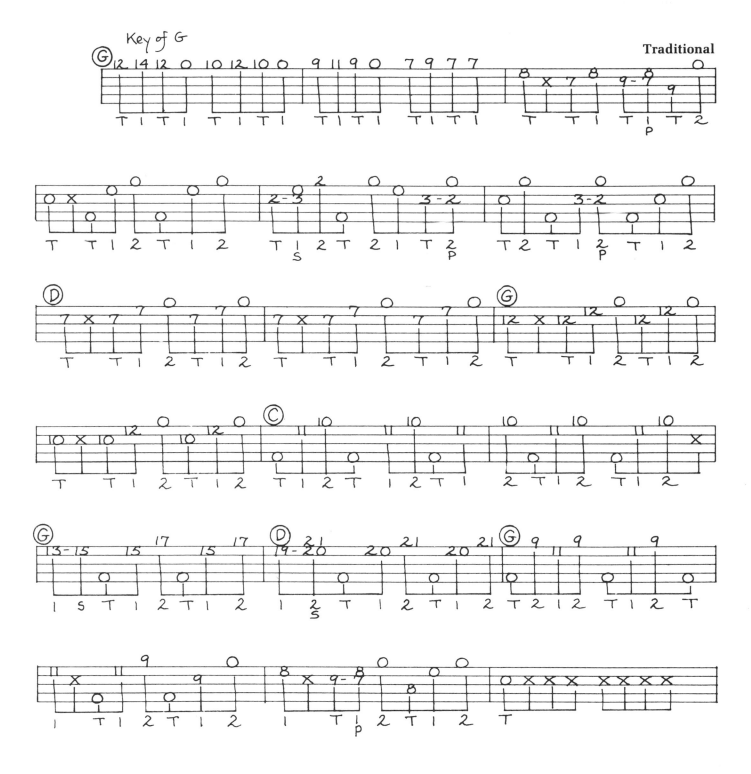

When You and I Were Young, Maggie

J.A. Butterfield

Key of G

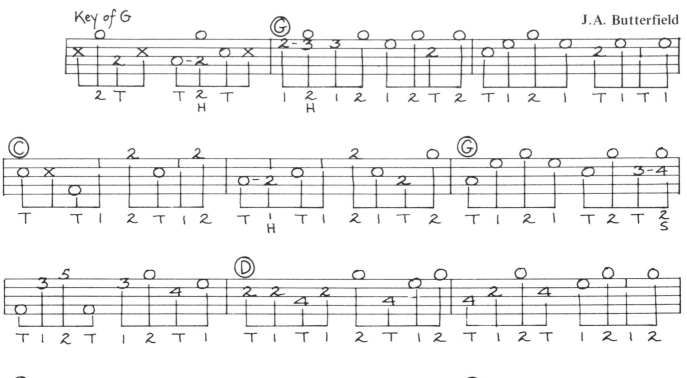

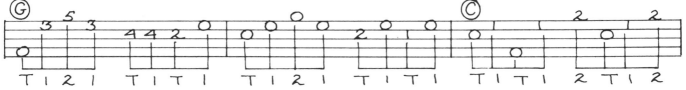

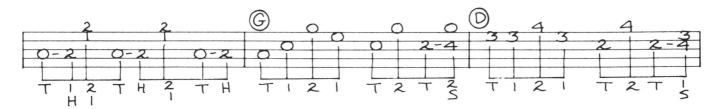

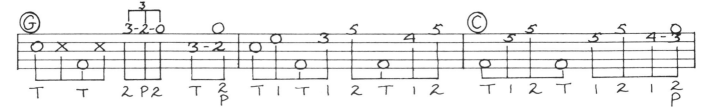

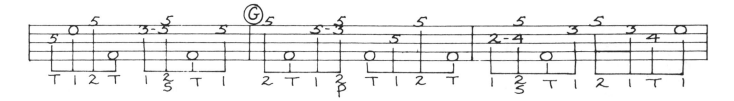

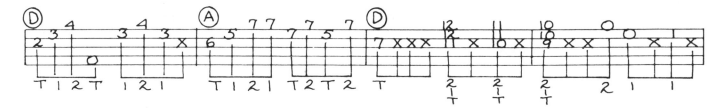

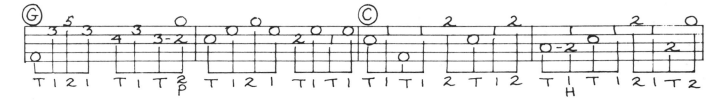

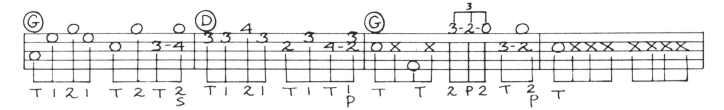

Ralph Stanley

Ralph Stanley appears to be a fairly reserved man on stage, but through his haunting vocals and lonesome banjo, he is able to communicate his life experiences directly and movingly to the listener. Music that touches that deeply has to have strong childhood roots. Ralph's are in the hills and earth of his native Virginia. "In the summertime, well, we lived on a small farm near McClure and we usually had our days cut out for us—raising and gardening, corn, cutting and putting up hay, and we always kept milk and livestock, horses, hogs. We had to feed them in the mornings and afternoons. And for a pastime we would hunt some, maybe go fishing or swimming."

Ralph's father worked in a sawmill and his mother was an accomplished banjo picker. In fact, hers was the first music Ralph heard. "She played the old-time style. I call it the clawhammer, you know, didn't use any picks, the way that I play some of the tunes now such as 'Shout Little Luly' and 'Little Birdie.' I listened to her and picked it up by myself. The first tune I learned was 'Shout Little Luly' and I went from there. That was probably '38 or '39." Ralph also played a two-finger style that he picked up from some of the other banjo players in the area. Soon, though, he was exposed to three-finger picking via radio. He would listen in the mornings before the day's work was begun and hear Snuffy Jenkins and later, Bill Monroe's hot new banjo player, Earl Scruggs. "I wanted to get it, but I wanted to get it as much different as I could. I didn't try to listen to a record or play it like anybody. I just wanted to get that finger roll and use it myself the way I heard it."

By 1946, Ralph had truly developed his own personalized banjo style. That October, he got a chance to try it out with his brother Carter on a small radio station, WNVA, in Norton, Virginia. But after only a month they decided to move to Bristol, Tennessee. There they started "Farm and Fun Time," a show that introduced their music for the first time to the wide listening public. "We had an hour each day. It covered about five states around that part of the country. We played three or four years just in that area—North Carolina, West Virginia, Kentucky. Of course, we recorded at that time and our records (for Rich-R-Tone and Columbia) got out and we became known through records farther on out."

It's interesting that Ralph and Carter were really the first ones to adopt the new sound that Bill Monroe had forged with the circa 1945-48 *Bluegrass Boys* (which included Flatt and Scruggs, and Chubby Wise). Although in those days the generic term bluegrass hadn't been coined, recordings from 1947 show that the Stanleys had fully integrated that Monroe sound with their own style.

You see, the Stanley Brothers started before Flatt and Scruggs, and they were with Bill Monroe at that time. We started '46 and I guess it was '48 when they started. Scruggs came up to Bristol where we were playing. I'd say just a couple months before he and Flatt left Bill. And I believe he stayed around with us maybe a week and went on three or four personal appearances with us. I believe he might have played a tune on the show. Of course, I guess he was just feeling the territory out, because they came there and started on "Farm and Fun Time" pretty shortly after they left Bill.

Of all the bluegrass bands that have proliferated since the late forties the *Stanley Brothers* was one of the most stable. "We played all the time except four or five months. I was in a car wreck [in 1951] and got knocked out and while I was recuperating Carter played a while with Bill Monroe, maybe four or six months. Other than that we played continuously together from '46 to '66" [the year of Carter's death].

In those years, and in the years following, many superb musicians, among them Mike Seeger, George Shuffler, Curly Sechler, Bobby Osborne, Larry Sparks, and Roy Lee Centers, became *Clinch Mountain Boys*. In addition to making some incredible music, these bands added numerous songs to the bluegrass repertoire, including such originals as "How Mountain Girls Can Love," "Love Me, Darling, Just Tonight," "Think of What You've Done," and—perhaps their best known tune—"Clinch Mountain Backstep." Ralph explains how he came to write "Clinch Mountain."

Well, I just mixed some tunes together on that, "Pretty Polly" and "Liza Jane." I just got to thinking, one time I was playing around, I'd play a little of this one, a little of that one, just put two or three together and come out with what I have with it. If you'll notice the way I trip the first string on "Clinch Mountain Backstep" . . . later on some banjo pickers, I don't know exactly what they call it. I call it the Yankee banjo picking. You know what I mean—what Bill Keith come out with. It's got a touch of that in it. The way I trip that string, it's not like it but it could've started from something, like that.

The old-time sound that's at the heart of "Clinch Mountain Backstep" and many other Stanley tunes just comes naturally to Ralph. "I think it's a gift that people get." As such, he wants to keep it as pure and strong as possible. At the same time, he leaves room for fresh material and innovation in his music. "I think you can learn something new every day. If something comes to you that you can't do it, well I'll do that, which I think would be good if it does. And fooling around with an instrument, you can always get a little something new if you try."

Style

Ralph's childhood had a strong effect on his banjo style. His mother's clawhammer renditions of the old songs, and his physical environment, the beautiful high ridges and narrow valleys of southwestern Virginia, were important as spiritual inputs for his music. With the more practical addition of modern Scruggs techniques, his playing crystallized into a spare and direct style firmly planted in bluegrass, but tinged by the less complex old-time sounds. "I think it's a little more plainer. In other words, it sticks right to the tune. I play as close or closer than anybody. It's just the way the melody is exactly." You can hear in "Pretty Polly" and "Little Maggie" that Ralph is able to pick out the literal melody without depending heavily on Scruggs licks. Those that he does use become part of the tune, rather than filler between phrases. This creates a more integrated sound—one which reveals the essential beauty of each song.

The real key to Ralph's style, though, is in the right hand. Except for an occasional syncopated note placed unexpectedly in a forward roll, he has a very straightforward rhythmic conception. The melody falls either on the onbeat (first and fifth notes of the measure), or on the offbeat (third and seventh notes of the measure), and rarely in between. Also, Ralph limits himself to a small variety of rolls: forward, backward, and thumb-to-middle-finger are the only ones in these two tunes. The T1T2 roll, which seems to produce a more updated sound, is missing entirely.

One of the most distinctive features of Ralph's style is the crisp banjo tone he gets by picking practically on top of the bridge. It's a strong, rough sound, and perhaps more than any other aspect of his style, it captures the feelings of determination, loneliness, and hardship which are at the heart of his music.

Pretty Polly

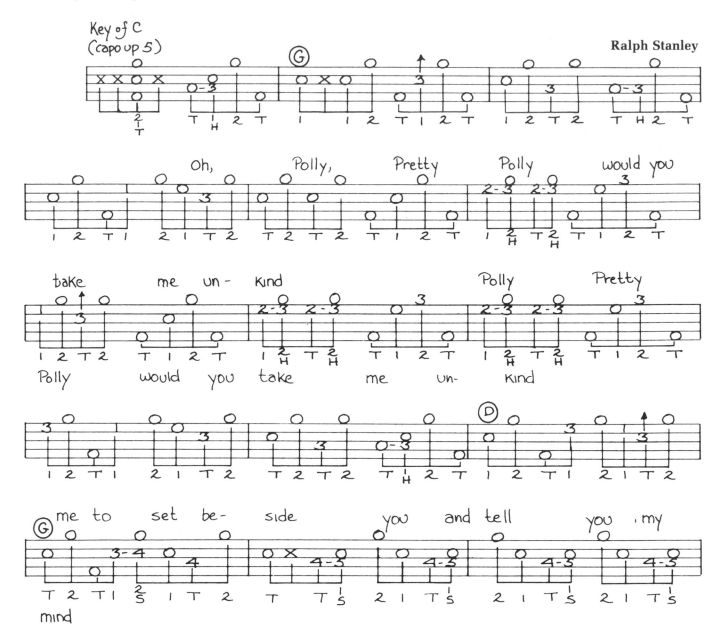

Little Maggie

capo 5
Key of C

Ralph Stanley

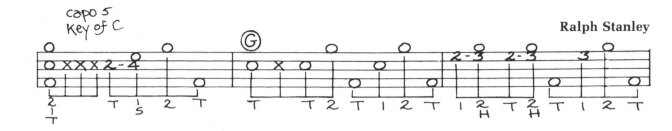

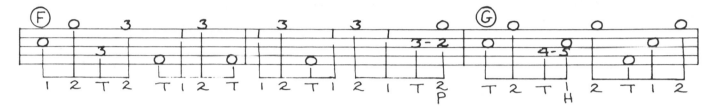

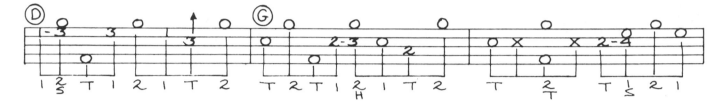

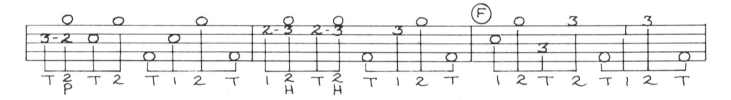

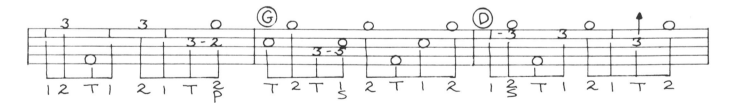

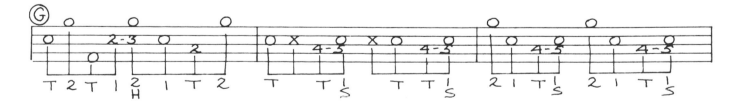

Sonny Osborne

The Osborne Brothers. L to R: Bobby Osborne, Sonny Osborne and Dale Sledd.

The exciting music that Scruggs, Reno and Stanley were creating quickly inspired a second generation of pickers to adopt the new banjo style. Among them was a youth who would play a large part in modernizing and popularizing the sound of Bluegrass—Sonny Osborne.

Sonny was born on October 29, 1937, in the small coal mining town of Hyden, Kentucky. From that moment on he was immersed in country music. Proximity to Tennessee allowed the Osbornes to pick up the sounds of the Grand Ole Opry on the family's battery radio. In addition, Sonny's father, a farmer and schoolteacher, played clawhammer banjo. "It was one of those old things without a back on it," Sonny recalls. "My Dad would sit around playing the banjo. He also played a little fiddle and a little guitar. So there was always instruments around as far as I can remember."

In 1941 the Osborne family moved to a farm outside of Dayton, Ohio. There Sonny's older brother Bobby discovered bluegrass music (known in those days as hillbilly music). Bobby was particularly impressed with Earl Scruggs' playing on "Cumberland Gap" and perhaps some of his enthusiasm was transmitted to Sonny. Larry Richardson, a banjo player who was passing through Dayton, provided further inspiration. He gave Sonny his first opportunity to hear live three-finger picking. "I wasn't interested in it because I was really in hot putsuit of a football or baseball career at that time. I was eleven

years old. But that always kind of stuck in my mind, the way he played that thing with his fingers." This fascination was soon translated into a desire to own a banjo. Since his father refused to lend financial support at first, he developed a knack for working things out in his head. For instance, he would sit in study hall thinking through Ralph Stanley's break to "Sweethearts in Heaven." Soon, though, his father relented, a banjo was procured and Sonny took his first lesson. As it happened, he played more proficiently than his teacher did, so he turned instead to records and radio shows to hone his technique. "That's where I spent my time—in front of a record player. Mainly the Scruggs records because they would be coming out all the time. I've worn more than one of them completely white." In addition to listening to Scruggs' playing, Sonny was absorbing the music of Don Reno, Larry Richardson, and Rudy Lyle (Bill Monroe's banjo player during the early fifties).

At this time, Bobby moved away from home and Sonny was left to do the farm chores. He usually worked from dawn to midnight plowing and discing before returning home to practice banjo on the back porch swing until 4:30 the next morning. This regimen continued for quite a while, and he soon became competent enough to play a few local jobs.

In the summer of 1951 Sonny landed his first professional work—a short stint with the *Lonesome Pine Fiddlers*. This band included his brother Bobby, Jimmy Martin, and the *Cline Brothers*, Ezra and Charlie. In November of that year, however, Bobby went into the Marines and Sonny and Jimmy headed back to Ohio.

In the fall Sonny returned to high school and remained relatively dormant until the summer of 1952. Then in July, he and Jimmy Martin took a fateful trip to Bill Monroe's country music park in Bean Blossom, Indiana. They arrived to find Monroe fronting an abbreviated band consisting of himself and Charley Cline. "He would have people leave him and then he would just go and work with one guy until somebody else would come along. So Jimmy asked Bill if he could go back to work with him (Martin had previously been a *Bluegrass Boy* in early 1951) and Bill said, 'Yeah.' Then he asked if I could go to work with him too and he said, 'Yeah, might as well.' " Monroe's offhand decision to include Sonny in his band was to have a profound effect on the young boy's future. From playing local jobs around Dayton, Sonny was suddenly thrust into a professional music career—and this at the age of fourteen.

The week after the Bean Blossom trip, Jimmy and Sonny headed for Nashville in Jimmy's 1940 Chrysler. In those days before interstates it was a tedious ride, but not without its humorous aspects. "We picked up this hitchhiker. He was in the service, and I guess the old boy was cold 'cause it was spring. We drove him maybe seventy-five miles and we had a flat, so this old boy voluteered to get out and fix it. When he fixed the flat he went in this restaurant to wash his hands and Jimmy says, 'Lets go.' I said, 'We can't leave that old boy.' He said, 'Well then we're even. We took him about seventy-five miles and he fixed our flat for us.' We did, we cut out."

Once in Nashville, the two checked into the Tulane Hotel, the site of most of the recording activity in town. Many of the Opry regulars used the studio there, including Monroe. In fact, within a day or two after arriving (July 18, 1952), Sonny had recorded eight tunes as a *Bluegrass Boy*, including "Footprints in the Snow," "In the Pines," and "Little Girl and the Dreadful Snake." Surprisingly, this was the first chance Monroe had to hear Sonny play.

A few days later Sonny found himself on the stage of the Grand Ole Opry. "The first thing I did on the Opry I remember quite well. It was "Rawhide," and that's a bad thing to put a thirteen-year-old kid to playing right off the bat. My knees were actually shaking. You know, you're standing around and there's Ernest Tubb, Hank Williams and Roy Acuff. I was literally scared to death." The simple fact was that Sonny was a green player. "Monroe had had a couple of bad musicians and in me he had another one, a guy that really couldn't play. I was probably the worst up to that time to be with him 'cause I didn't have any experience so I didn't really have a chance."

Still, it was a giant step ahead for Sonny's career. When he returned home after a summer of playing,

he got together with Enos Johnson and Carlos Brock, two local musicians, to do some sides for Gateway Records. Most of the tunes recorded were "covers," or copies of popular songs originally done by Monroe and Flatt and Scruggs. These were then hawked by mail order over various midwestern radio stations. Ironically, the tune that sold the most copies (67,000) was a Sonny Osborne original, "Sunny Mountain Chimes." It was obvious now that the ball was rolling. So Sonny decided to quit the tenth grade for the somewhat precarious life of a musician. He rejoined Monroe in April of 1953 with the idea of staying indefinitely. In September, though, Bobby got out of the service, Sonny left the *Bluegrass Boys*, and the *Osborne Brothers* were back in business.

It was a modest reunion at first, featuring just the two of them—Sonny on banjo and Bobby on guitar and mandolin. Soon, though, they were recording more "covers" for Gateway, and in the summer of 1954 Jimmy Martin joined the Osbornes to record such classics as "20-20 Vision" and "Save It, Save It" for RCA. As great as this band was, personal chemistry interfered, conflicts arose and the band was dissolved. Sonny, however, wasn't worried in the least. "I was starting to realize Bobby might be the best singer in the world right then anyway. I figured he'd take me to the Opry. That was the goal, even right then." The ten years it took to get there, though, were not always easy.

After a brief stay in West Virginia, Sonny and Bob returned to Dayton to slug it out on the rugged bar circuit. Red Allen was also working this terrain, and in 1956 the three decided to join forces. Although they quickly developed an amazing sound, their music did not always soothe the savage beast. "Red got into it with some guy one night. The guy hit him and, boy, Red took a beer bottle about half full of beer and broke it over that guy's nose. But the old boy came in the next night and he was just bandaged like a mummy, but he came back. You've got to give him that." Fortunately, things soon took a turn for the better. The group signed with MGM Records and the WWVA Jamboree.

The first MGM hit for Osborne, Osborne and Allen was "Ruby." The song featured Bobby's crystal tenor and Sonny's Rubenesque D-tuned banjo. Although this opened new doors for the group—including a tour with the wildly popular Johnny Cash—MGM only printed up a limited number of copies of the record and when those were gone, that was it. This was a result of MGM's reluctance to gamble on a country group in the face of the growing popularity of rock 'n' roll. Nevertheless, Sonny, Bob and Red continued to make records, including "Once More," which was released in 1958. This was the first tune to feature the Osbourne's new "pile under" harmony which featured Bobby's lead voice on top with baritone below that and a low tenor buried still further underneath. Soon after this recording Red left the band and the group became known simply as the *Osborne Brothers*.

In 1960 Sonny and Bob became the first bluegrass band to play for a university audience with their performance at Antioch College. This was just a foreshadowing of the milestones to come. In 1963 they signed with Decca records, which in turn led to the long sought slot on the Grand Ole Opry. Along with the move to Decca went a change in sound. "I got hold of a thing called "Up This Hill and Down," and that was really the first thing that opened the door to disc jockeys because it wasn't just out and out bluegrass. It was kind of bluesy and a little bit of rock." Though this wasn't a big hit for the Osbornes, it sold respectably. Then in 1967 they had their monster—"Rocky Top." With sales of eighty thousand in the first month their success was assured.

Soon pianos, pedal steels and even string sections began popping up on their albums and the charge was made by traditionalists that the Osbornes had sold out. To add insult to injury, Sonny and Bob amplified their own instruments in 1969 so that they could better compete with the louder country bands in the coliseum package shows. During this period Sonny actually had his resonator padlocked to his flange to keep the details of his pickup a secret. Then Sonny's patented 6-string banjo was added to their list of innovations. "I started thinking about that about 1967 and it always bothered me that you would get to a certain place in a tune and you couldn't play the actual tune. You had to play some kind of messed-up lick to get away from a low note in a tune. So I got a thing about adding a string to it." By now the din from the defenders of the faith was deafening. In a state of obvious exasperation Sonny fired off this letter to *Bluegrass Unlimited*:

> *"If we are guilty, as accused, of discarding bluegrass, we would lay down our banjos and mandolins and pick up violins and trumpets!!! and there would be the death of bluegrass. (By we, I don't mean just the Osborne Brothers. I'm talking about every outfit who has tried this same thing.)*
> *"No matter how you flavor it, boil it, fluoridate it, purify it, bottle it, aerate it, coffee it, tea it, freeze it, or use it—water is still water. The same with guitar, banjo, mandolin, fiddle and bass—no matter, bluegrass is still bluegrass."**

Ultimately, the Osbornes were waging a battle on two fronts. While trying to open the ears of the bluegrass world to more pop-oriented sounds, they were fighting simultaneously to get bluegrass onto the pop country charts. This latter battle was hard fought but brought them enough financial security to free them from the grueling road work most bluegrass musicians have to put up with all their lives.

Two hundred and ninety-one thousand miles in twenty-six months. That was '70 and '71. You know what made that so bad was the pressure. We were playing these things where we were competing with the biggest names in country music. The best spot in a coliseum package show is to close the first half because everybody's really ready. And we finally got to the point where we were doing that on all of them and most of the time got a standing ovation. I'll tell you, that's competing. That's why I'm so proud of what we do. We got into their game and they laughed at us for doing it. But we beat them at their own game and I really love that type of thing. I like the fight. But it's kind of over now, and I'm glad it is because we're just picking what we want to do now.

Style

Sonny is as innovative a banjo player as you're likely to find today. He achieves his sound by employing blues licks, a free right hand and a healthy respect for the Scruggs tradition. "Scruggs records. If you get your right hand to do what his did from 1949 to '56, you can do anything there is to do. He did all of it." Even so, Sonny is not tied to Earl's sound. "In '57 I heard Scruggs miss a thing with his right hand and I thought then and there, before there wasn't anything to go on at all, I better find me a way to play—and I started just getting away from the direct copy of Scruggs and just started basing everything on that, but then going to other areas too. And I started doing steel licks, piano licks, and horns and anything I can hear."

Interestingly, Sonny avoids melodic licks like the plague. "I truly believe chromatics has hurt banjo playing as far as young kids playing it. I don't know how to play it, but it must be easier to play than just the old hard driving things. I don't like it at all. I don't see that there's any place for it in the type of music we're doing, anyway."

The right hand: "That's all of it. You can do anything, but if you don't have a good right hand you're sunk to begin with."

On constructing a break: "When I first start a break there's nothing on my mind. I'm just gonna play it and then I'll think, well in the fourth line it would be good to do this. Then I'll start thinking back in the third line of what pattern I have to be in to get out of that into the fourth line. So I don't really think of what I'm playing at the time. I'm trying to think maybe two lines ahead."

On originality: "Playing and what you get out of an instrument is just what you hear. It's how you want to hear it come out. I really think that's a hang-up for young people that's playing today. They don't know what they want to hear coming out of it. They just want to play something they see a guy playing. They want to do that too. Even back when I was fourteen years old, I knew exactly what I wanted to hear."

On working out breaks: For "Up This Hill and Down" I had heard some things on a Buck Owens record of years gone by and we were in the studio doing it, and like I live here (Hendersonville, Tennessee), and where we recorded was at Bradley's

*Bluegrass Unlimited, June 1967.

Barn, which is some twenty miles from here. All the stuff that I figured out has been between here and the Barn. You really get psyched to go and pick, and between here and and there I'd figure out a lot of things. It became a ritual. I'd always try to go by myself, where I could really think. And a lot of the stuff that I've done, too, has been right out here cutting this grass, because I do all this myself and, boy, you can really think sitting on a tractor. I don't know why you can, but I can anyway."

Rocky Top

Boudleaux and Felice Bryant

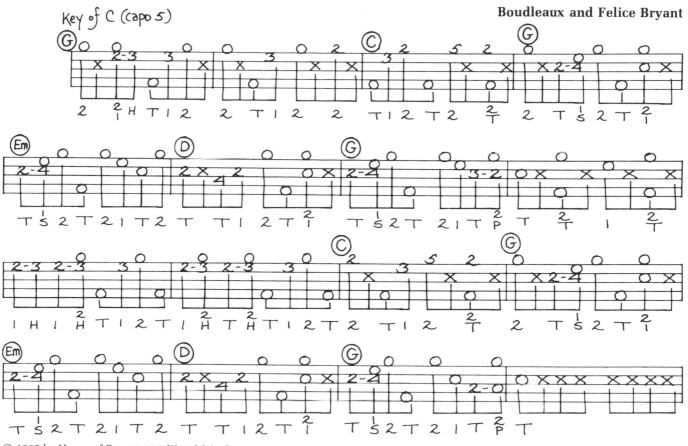

Rueben

Sonny Osborne

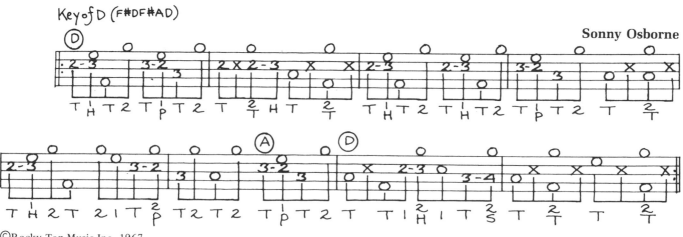

Cumberland Gap

Key of G
Part A

Traditional

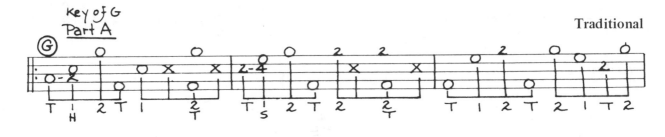

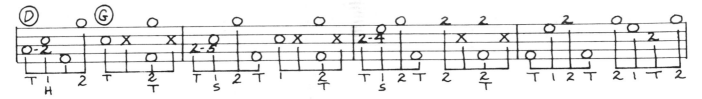

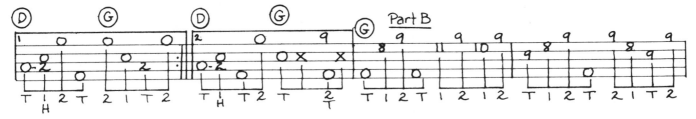

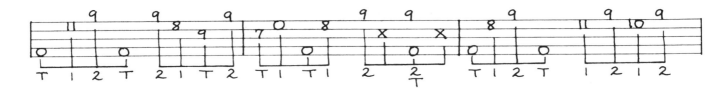

50

Allen Shelton

Jim and Jesse and the *Virginia Boys* at the Newport Folk Festival, 1973, with Jim Buchanan (fiddle) and Allen Shelton (banjo).

"I guess I've just had different ideas. Maybe they were too different from what everyone else was playing. I thought there must be something else to play besides 'Foggy Mountain Breakdown.'" And indeed there was. At a time (mid-to-late fifties) when most banjo pickers were content to work up the latest Earl Scruggs instrumental, Allen Shelton was going beyond the conventional bluegrass repertoire into jazz and pop standards, in his search for new material. With one ear he seemed to be listening to Scruggs and Reno, and with the other, Les Paul and Mary Ford. Tunes such as "Bye Bye Blues," "Five Foot Two, Eyes of Blue," and "Sweet Georgia Brown"—unusual material for a man with traditional roots—found their way into his playing.

Allen was born in 1936 near Reidsville, North Carolina. "My parents farmed and they had a radio. And the music my Dad played was our entertainment. He played most any instrument, better, I'd say, on guitar and banjo. That was when I was fifteen, in '49 or '50. He started straight with bluegrass. In fact, he brought a banjo home to learn to play and that's when I got into it."

Radio programming at that time also had a lot to offer. "We'd come in from the field and we could pick up WPTF Raleigh. I could get the Flatt and Scruggs local radio show every day and then I could just flip the dial and get the Reno and Smiley radio show and they were really putting down some good music. I liked Scruggs's hard-driving music and I liked Reno's fantastic backup and real fast chord structures, and I liked several of his instrumentals." Reno was also doing some of his jazzier licks back then, and some of that rubbed off on Allen. "Like 'I Know You're Married But I Love You Still.' The jumping that he did on that I loved. Of course, I couldn't do it."

With some of these early influences integrated into his own music, Allen landed his first professional job with Jim Eanes in 1950. He had been with Jim for six months when he got a call from Mac Wiseman, who was working on the 'Old Dominion Barndance' out of Richmond. During Allen's stay, they recorded seven sides at the Tulane Hotel in Nashville, among them one of Mac's future trademarks, "Love Letters in the Sand." The time spent with Mac was also valuable for Allen because it gave him a chance to develop power and solidity in his right hand. "He didn't carry a bass and he'd play very little rhythm on the guitar. And if a hard-driving style was ever needed, there is where you had to put it."

When Mac decided to move the band from Richmond to Raleigh, Allen went to work for *Hack Johnson and the Tennesseeans* and almost ended up playing with Reno and Smiley in the process. "They

51

were on the 'Old Dominion Barndance' and Hack Johnson was too. Reno would fall out on the stage and do 'Muleskinner Blues' and eat it up on guitar. He'd come ask me to play background on the banjo. Well I thought it sounded great and he must've thought so too. So he talked about hiring me. But at that time Reno and Smiley had a swinging band— Mack Magaha and John Palmer, so it didn't happen.''

After playing with Hack, Allen went back to Jim Eanes. ''At that time I learned to play most of the requests for Scruggs stuff and the most requested Reno stuff, or anybody's. But unless they were requested I'd try to pick something commercial that I thought they'd like. I used to do stuff like 'Bill Bailey Won't You Please Come Home.' ''

Back then Don Reno was one of the only other banjoists exploring music outside the bluegrass realm. ''When I was working for Jim Eanes out of Martinsville, only fifty miles from Roanoke, Reno was on Roanoke and he could hear me and I could hear him. I thought it kind of odd, you know, as soon as I worked out 'Under the Double Eagle' and played it two or three times, just a month or two later it came out on a King record with Reno. Of course, it was completely different the way he did it. I don't hold any hard feelings.''

The time spent with Eanes was really a time of experimentation for Allen. ''We worked three square dances a week, solid, and that's four or five hours of straight playing. Somebody had to take those breaks. That's really where what everybody calls my weird backup stuff came from. Before then I was doing the same thing everybody else did. But during the square dances they don't care if you make a mistake, so you try anything.''

In this search for new sounds, Allen began to adapt steel guitar licks to the banjo. ''I always loved pedal steel. I've even got a record I made where I had pedals on my banjo—an old Jim Eanes Starday record called 'Your Old Standby.' The pedal was mounted on the tailpiece. The banjo was tuned to D. You'd hit the pedals and it automatically pulled both strings to G. You'd use the Scruggs tuners to tune it down and then hit the pedal to bring it back to G.''

In the late fifties, Allen became friendly with Bobby Thompson. ''We used to get together and jam at every chance. Bobby was working with Jim and Jesse and he'd done several Starday records with them. But he got fouled up someway and pulled active duty in the army. That's when they called me and I went to work with them. That was in '60 and I was with them six years until 1966.''

During those six years, Allen became one of the most respected banjoists in the country. On recordings such as ''Stony Creek'' and ''Standing on the Mountain,'' his style was a model of invention, taste, and drive. The rest of the band was equally strong. Jesse's original crosspicking approach to the mandolin, Jimmy Buchanan's sinewy fiddle lines, and Jim, Jesse, and Don McCann's fluid trio singing were an unbeatable combination. McCann played rhythm guitar, but also provided one-half of the double

banjo sound that Jim and Jesse featured on a couple of songs. ''He was playing in straight open G and I tuned in D and clamped and hit the C [fifth] fret and that would put me in G with the D tuning. And almost note for note, every note that he'd make, I'd make and it would be tenor harmony. You can try that and it works.''

The years spent with Jim and Jesse were fulfilling for Allen, in part because the band sounded so good, and also because he was given a lot of space to develop and perfect his style. ''I felt free as a breeze. I can honestly say they never once told me what to play.''

Unfortunately, in 1966 a conflict arose which ultimately caused Allen to leave the band.

> I had a chance to record for Victor and I had three of the songs picked out. I had the idea to combine banjo with the Nashville Symphony and Chet Atkins liked it. We were going to do this more or less standard jazz type stuff. Jim and Jesse didn't go for it at all. They were paying me straight salary and I was working straight for them. Whether I played a show or not I'd draw my money. Actually they liked the music. Oh, Jesse would have had me record the same stuff for them. But that was one thing that started the strain. But that's all in the past. We're still good friends.

When Allen first left Jim and Jesse, he gave up music to work in a machine shop. This was followed by a stay in New Orleans, where he learned welding. He has since returned to Tennessee, and although he still works in the building trades, he's found time to return to his music via recordings. Happily, his playing is as fresh and innovative today as it was in the fifties and sixties. ''It was my opinion in those days they were trying to limit the banjo. In other words you only wanted a banjo in a fast bluegrass tune and nothing else. I think it can be played in anything and folks these days have proved that, and I thought that all along. I guess that's just the way I think it ought to be. That's the way I hear it.''

Style

In keeping with the philosophy that less is more, Allen learned early on how to get the maximum effect out of the smallest number of notes. For instance, in the *A* parts of ''Sourwood Mountain'' and ''Ridge Runner,'' he works with only six different notes. By rearranging them in all sorts of inventive ways, he manages to fill those sections with a lot of exciting music. This is a direct result of his fantastic right-hand technique: he uses rolls rather than left-hand fingerings to determine the sound. The following is a combination of the first, fifth, and part of the sixth bars of ''Ridge Runner.'' They show you the number of ways Allen can vary four notes.

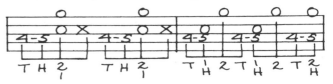

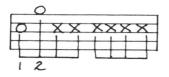

In addition to his skillful use of these shifting rolls, Allen has created a number of set right-hand licks which have become standards of the repertoire. There's this common one from *Part A* of "Shelton Special":

And try this steel oriented lick which occupies the second B flat in the *B* part of "Ridgerunner":

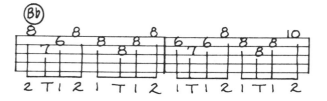

Both of the above are practically begging to be added to your playing.

As for the left hand, Allen was one of the first to bring blues notes to the banjo. Take this D lick, which is similar to the one he used for the end of "Standing on the Mountain" in the early sixties:

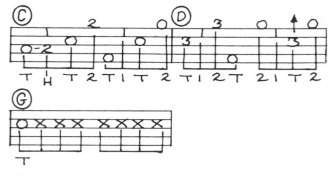

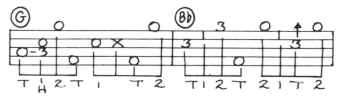

The bluesey *B* section of Shelton Special features essentially the same lick.

In his search for new sounds, Allen has been drawn to a number of tunes with unusual chord changes. For instance, "Stoney Creek," which he originally recorded with Jim and Jesse, begins in A, and then jumps to F for the *B* part. Similar in feel to this is Jesse's own "Ridge Runner," which kicks off in G and winds up in B-flat. "Shelton Special," though a bit more down to earth, is also written in two different keys: D and G. All of these tunes stray slightly from tradition, but Allen turns them into pure bluegrass and fills them with a warmth, bounce, and drive that few others can match.

Ridge Runner

Jesse McReynolds

Shelton Special

Allen Shelton

Sourwood Mountain

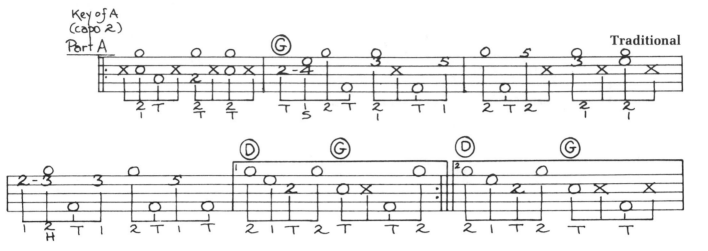

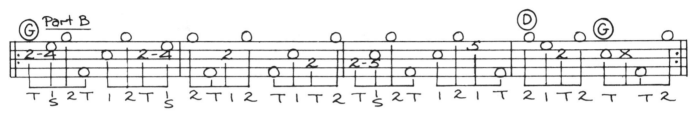

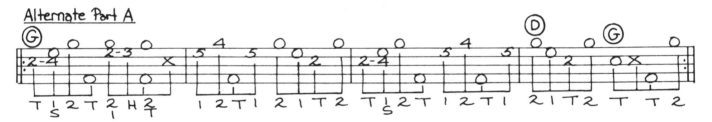

56

Bill Keith

L to R: David Grisman, Tony Rice, Bill Keith and David Schwartz, 1976.

After Don Reno's single-string approach had been absorbed into the bluegrass mainstream, there was a fallow period preceding the next major stylistic development. Although Don had given banjo players a new freedom by devising a way to play note-for-note melodies, the instrument still had limitations.

In March of 1963, Boston-born Bill Keith became the first northerner to join Bill Monroe's *Bluegrass Boys.* Within a couple of weeks of joining, he had recorded a number of tunes with Monroe that would permanently alter the character of bluegrass banjo. Two of these, "Sailor's Hornpipe" and "Devil's Dream," featured Bill's new melodic style; a style that, for the first time, made it possible to play fiddle tunes note for note, smoothly, and with ease. (In all fairness, it should be mentioned that Bobby Thompson had been independently working on the same basic style a few years before Keith appeared on the scene.) Thanks to Bill Monroe's popularity in the South, and his discovery by the northern folk revivalists, Keith was able to communicate his new ideas to a wide audience.

It was those new ideas that enabled us to look at the banjo from a totally different perspective. Now, in the following interview, Bill talks about expanding the improvisational and compositional potential of the instrument still further. The concepts he talks about may even help you unlock some musical doors of your own.

TONY: *Are you conscious of what you're playing?*
BILL: *Well, there's a lot of choice involved. There was an attitude that was a pretty recent development in the last year or two that I've been trying to put into action, and this is to keep breaking down the length of the unit that you think about. It could be an entire tune in the melodic style. Say you learn the thing and if somewhere you make a mistake playing, you get out of gear because you're thinking about the tune in terms of long phrases. Instead, you could think about ideas that are one measure long and that's your building block. And use that every time you have a D7 measure and it goes to G and then you have a choice between three G licks you can use to fill that measure. That's a size building block that's recognizable so your playing is easily broken down into sections by the listener. It's important, I think, as a way to improvise to continually shorten the length of the phrase that you're using so that there are more decisions necessary, more choices because you're working with smaller*

blocks. And finally, when this is reduced to the shortest block you have to deal with, the decision factor gets to be a lot simpler, because after each note there are only two others available. At that point, if you can think that fast, and improvise at that level, then you do have complete flexibility to make anything happen that comes into your head.

T: That's probably one of the main limitations of bluegrass banjo playing in general. It's so lick oriented.

B: That's true. But it's not like playing a melodic lick on, say, a wind instrument. If you discount changing registers with the special little key that lets you jump up an octave. But if you play the continuous melody notes on one of those, going up and down the scales, it's like writing, where each letter is connected to the next one. On the banjo, it seems that it's not writing in that manner because the notes are often on a different string, different both right and left hand formations. There isn't, I don't think, intrinsically as much improvisational freedom. Things are more apt to come out as licks. But I really think that's more the attitude of the player. If he can successfully break down the size of the blocks and use them in recognizable ways, then his playing will seem to change from one of just licks that are repeated in places where you need them, to more imaginative playing, more surprising playing for the listener.

T: How could one do that?

B: By analyzing your own playing. Where is my choice? Did I make a choice or did that just come out? Is there something better to play at that point? Would any change be better than playing something I've already played dozens of times before, trying another idea? Basically, if you just look at the pieces of what that's made of and how the idea is contained in the long phrase, then you'll get ideas of how you can convey the same harmonic idea with different notes and different positions, with a difference in rhythm.

T: Using different right hand rolls.

B: Right. It's really one thing to just change the right hand using the same chord position. You get something, sure. But it's really when you work something out that's very carefully chosen, well, using a left hand idea that may only be useable in that place. That's where you're really refining an idea to express it individualistically. It pertains to something I've worked on before. Having three or four or six or eight ways of doing D measures that would go into the G. Usually two measures in a row. When I was learning those, it was important to get all sixteen notes [in banjo tablature there are usually sixteen notes in two measures] to come out in a row that were the way I had written them on paper. What's more important is to use any part of those and rearrange the elements. If the elements are eight units long, then we have two possible arrangements of them; and if they are four units long, then you've got twenty-four, or one times two

times three times four, or whatever number of possibilities; and if the phrases are only two notes long, then there's a stack of them. They're no longer the same old licks. It's just using something you already know how to do, reorganized in a different way so it has different potential. I guess what makes something easier to learn is just being able to convince yourself that you already know how to do it. It's just a question of showing yourself that it's as easy to do as everything else that you're sure you can do, because once you've played for a few years, you've probably made every right hand motion that you'd ever have to know to play a classical style as well as bluegrass. If you organize the moves in the right sequence, then you're playing a completely other style.

One thing I think of in passing. I think it's really important to work on musical ideas without an instrument. I think it can be helpful to do things on paper. In certain ways, you can research chord positions on paper as well as on the instrument, sometimes very productively. And you can write tablature to a tune without an instrument. I once worked out all the tablature for a dozen different scales, all of which could be played in the G tuning without a capo or without changing the fifth string; just in an airport waiting for a plane, with a sheet of tablature paper. When you pick up an instrument, your tendency is to make some music and what you know comes out. What you don't know can't come out. I just think it's productive to think about music at times when you're not holding an instrument; to listen to tunes at any time you hear them with an analytical ear, and to immediately make some idea in progress on how that would fit on your instrument when you next are able to play it. One way to get around the limitations of your instrument is by not having it in your hand.

Style

"Morrison's Jig" and "Shenandoah Breakdown" represent two different aspects of Bill's music. "Morrison's Jig" involves the purely melodic style; "Shenandoah Breakdown," an original strain of Scruggs style interspersed with occasional melodics.

"Morrison's Jig" is Bill's arrangement of a traditional piece. He learned it from the French mandolinist Alain Stievel, who in turn learned it from fiddler Pierre Bensusan. Notice that it's in 6/8 time, which, for our purposes, indicates six notes per measure. Beyond that, there's nothing particularly unusual about the tune except for the fact that it's in A minor, a key not often heard on the banjo. As a result, even though you're playing out of standard positions, the sound is fresh. After you've gone through this a few times, you'll see that Part B is basically a variation of Part A, but moved up an octave. The only tricky thing to watch out for is the left-hand fingering for the second A minor chord in Part B. This is probably the easiest position to work out of for this passage.

Bill Monroe and the *Bluegrass Boys*, 1963. L to R: Bessie Lee Maudlin, Bill Monroe, Melissa Monroe, Joe Stuart, Bill Keith and Del McCoury.

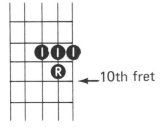

←10th fret

Technical considerations aside, this is a very pretty tune, and a good example of the "high, lonesome sound" of Ireland.

"Shenandoah Breakdown" was recorded by Bill on March 17, 1963, after he had been with the *Bluegrass Boys* for only a week or two. Since Bill Monroe couldn't remember the tune when it came time to record, he had to call up Joe Drumwright, the banjoist who had originally performed it with him, and have Joe play it over the phone to jog his memory.

I think this is one of Keith's nicest breaks. It's very thoughtfully wrought, and the execution is flawless. Bill weds his immaculate taste here with a high concentration of forward rolls to create a straight ahead, but original, bluegrass sound. For contrast, he sews this melodic lick seamlessly into the middle of *Part B.*

This is the real "hook" of the tune and is probably an ancestor of the endlessly descending Bobby Thompson runs that are so common today.

Morrison's Jig

Part A
Key of A minor

Traditional

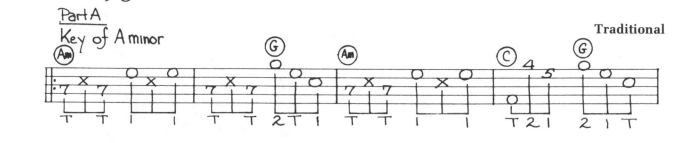

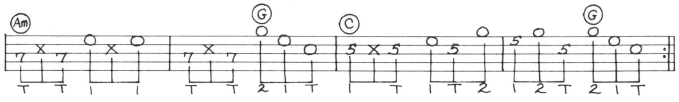

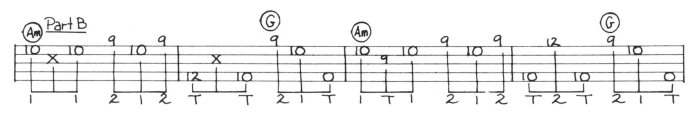

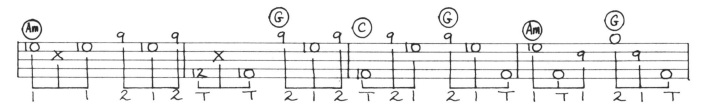

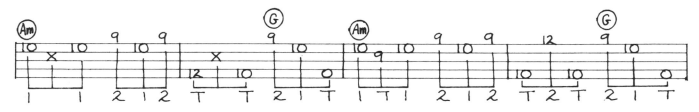

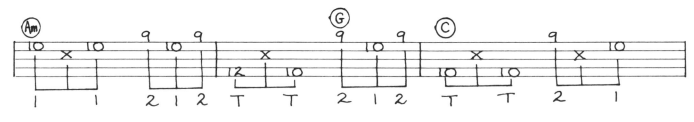

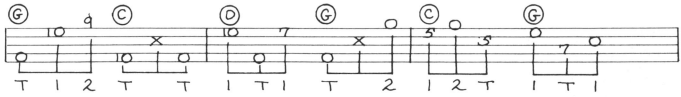

Shenandoah Breakdown

(capo 2)
Key of A

Bill Monroe

The Future

Butch Robins, Larry McNeely, and Pat Cloud represent all that's new in bluegrass banjo. Using standard techniques, they hear with fresh ears, and create music limited only by the boundaries of their own imaginations. They listen to jazz, rock, and the infinite for inspiration; and for grounding, tune in to tradition.

Butch Robins is the most conspicuously conscious of his debt to tradition. His first Rounder album contains old time fiddle tunes and a medley of Scruggs favorites. But with the aid of a dobro-banjo, extended rests, and atonal licks, he also comes up with his own experimental sound.

Larry McNeely is equally steeped in tradition, having spent his earlier years with Roy Acuff. How-ever, he too has arrived at a probingly original writing style.

Pat Cloud has undoubtedly stepped the furthest out on a limb by exchanging standard bluegrass licks almost entirely for a highly jazz oriented style.

There are, of course, other fine players searching for new sounds: Bela Fleck (Boston), John Lanford (Tulsa), and Pete Schwimmer (Bellingham, Washington) come immediately to my mind. But the number of people creating new music is still small. It is growing, though, and pretty soon the futurists of today will become the mainstreamers of tomorrow. Then someone even farther out will have to lead the way to the next future.

Butch Robins

Butch Robins is as comfortable with the strictly traditional styles as he is with the more modern "outside"—and I do mean outside—approaches to banjo. Perhaps this is a result of his chameleonlike career. It has included, on the one hand, regular Saturday night appearances on the "Grand Ole Opry" with Wilma Lee and Stoney Cooper; and on the other, a tour with Leon Russell as the *Newgrass Revival*'s bass player. Butch may not be well known to a lot of people, but he's been bouncing around the bluegrass world for the last ten years, adding his considerable talents to such varied recording ventures as Kenny Baker's *Baker's Dozen*, Ronnie Reno's solo album, and Leon Russell's *Hank's Back*. He may also be the world's foremost bluegrass philosopher. The following collection of thoughts, culled from a lengthy interview, will bear this out. This discussion was taped in the blurry early morning hours; in a candlelit room; in a small house behind Starday studios in Nashville. Butch was recording his first solo album for Rounder Records.

I hit an incredible high one year and went from the depths of real weird bad to playing three months on the Leon Russell tour with the Revival. Then there was a month in Las Vegas with Harry James. I was in a band that was part of that show. It sort of brought me down, though, because of the routine of it. It was just like any other computerized little job. Good charts, but the same every night, nobody'd jam on the charts. It was just too weird. But I thought it was good training. That was '72 probably. Those times there, each one was a new level. Like when I came off the Leon Russell stuff, I got to play with Buck White and it brought me back down to earth out of the rock n' roll. It was really a heavy trip playing some with Buck, because he's pure music and he lets you have incredible glimpses of that music. It's just fantastic, the high thing you get with him.

I started really listening to music that year, more than I ever had in my entire life. I was going to get a job with Clarence and Roland White, that's while they were in Sweden, and I heard that Alan Munde wasn't working regularly for them. Clarence just gave off incredible amounts of energy. It was real poetry in notes. I was really looking forward to going with them and a week before I was to start was the week Clarence died.

Then I got that job with Sam Bush, Courtney Johnson, Curtis Burch. I was in a situation there where every man knew his music inside of him. It was an equal share proposition. They just played strong, every one of them, and they just taught me how to start tapping what's inside of me to play. Before that I was always trying to play like sombody else.

The Revival taught me how to hear. How to listen out of inside of me. They were so strong, each one giving himself and they complimented each other and it was a complete freedom. And there were two or three times that each one of them gave completely and freely. Those nights we were so close together and thinking and felt each other so well that we knew how to play in order to complement each other's playing. Those were magnificent events in my life because there were times when we would come off the stage that I would be shaking. The thing that hit was an awareness, an awakening to music.

Curtis Burch could be the Vassar Clements of dobro players because he is so weird, that dobro talks for him.

Music is anything that can take an emotion out of you and transmit it in through your hands into that instrument and make it come out in notes and it's a concrete product in those notes for just maybe a split second. And it's something they get with one of their five senses and it goes in their ears and it just gets them up. That's what music is to me. The art in it is that it evokes an emotion in that person who receives it.

I think on the full moon my playing's going to be as crazy as hell and the other times right after that it's going to start being straight. It'll be straight for the first quarter, then it'll get mellow second quarter, then it'll get paranoid for the third quarter.

I met Jimmy Martin one Christmas and he knows a hell of a lot about banjo picking. I think a lot of J. D. Crowe's comes right directly from old Jimmy's tutoring. By George, he taught me how to keep a roll going. But it was something that I knew all along, the sound was in my head all along. He just showed me how to do it, how to keep it going, how to make it

melodic within a very simple way. He was the first one who really taught me about drive.

I just want somebody to recognize that I'm here and I'm a working human being. I am trying to make my soul. And the one thing in this life that makes me complete that I totally give to everybody around me is my music. It's the only means I've got to be a voice to be heard by people that I want to pick it up and I want to paint with it. I want to give them a product that's alive, that's trying to think about where it's going and aiming for something more on a spiritual level where you can reach and touch souls. That's what I want to do to an audience and I think about that.

Watch Bill Monroe's feet, watch him dance, watch the rhythm in his body. How stately it is, how sturdy it is. How tall he stands. The power. The older I get, the more I get attracted to him. The power and strength, and it's a mature strength. It's like taking all the best things. All that energy and youth and just adding on the maturity and wisdom of age. Putting all that together to splatter music out.

For the most part, Scruggs plays just damn nice, real straight, simple lines, like he always did. But they've matured, they've mellowed. You know there's much more tone, much more depth to them. That concentration on tone, it's taken some of the edge off his playing, but it's added to the richness and the fullness, such an amazing sound he gets out of the banjo. And it ain't all in that microphone. A lot of it's got to do with that man's right hand. Like I was brought up on the school of thinking it all had to do with the right hand. How much power you can lay into it with, or how soft you could play it and lay into it with, or how soft you could play it and still play with the punch, the drive. And I find I'm still having to revert to the one ultimate power, everything I've got in my hand. So when I get through with an overdub or a tune, my arm aches because I just have to put out on it. I've got to put out everything I've got. It's got to be on top of the music. Because if I'm scratching and crawling and I'm lagging behind, then that means I'm getting old on it. That means I'm dragging and I ain't going to have that. Because the spirit of my playing's always going to be young. This old boy's gonna age but the spirit inside me and the product I give people is timeless, is my soul itself.

Style

These next two tunes demonstrate the complete spectrum of Butch's talents: the heavy Scruggs influence, the melodics, and perhaps most important, his affinity for the avant garde.

The entire A part of "Monkey in the Garden" is a shock to the well-oiled bluegrass system as we know it. It starts reasonably enough with a very nice melodic lick but quickly falls into an abyss of six rests. The lick repeats and again falls in the chasm.

Then in the sixth bar the death blow is dealt as controlled mayhem breaks loose—strange notes, halting timing, and syncopated accents. To Ornette Coleman this might be child's play, but placed in the context of a chugging bluegrass rhythm section, it's heresy. Butch definitely likes to take chances and gives us all a good earstretching in the process.

From here on things normalize. *Part B* begins *à la* Allen Shelton with these two useful right-hand oriented licks.

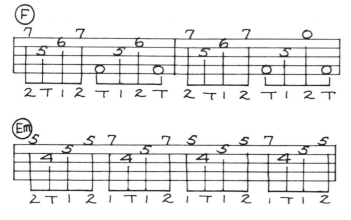

The last four bars of this section are pure Scruggs.

Part C is a melodic reworking of the opening theme, but without all the fireworks. The second to the last bar contains one more lick you can use; it's also borrowed from Allen Shelton.

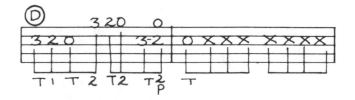

"T To The 7th Power" has a strong melodic influence and sounds . . . well, like Butch Robins. It's hard to trace roots here.

Part A has a tasty and jaunty melody which ends with a fairly difficult, syncopated transition into *Part B*. It will be easier if you have the record for this one. *Part B* consists of a circle of fourths (B, E, A, D: each of these chords is separated by the interval of a fourth), and relies pretty much on fixed chord positions. The ending of this section is a crazy quilt of atonal triplets and, like *Part A* of "Monkey," is pure Robins.

Butch has an amazing command of all banjo styles, including a deep understanding of the subtleties of the Scruggs sound. But I think his own explorations will be most important in setting a high standard for the future growth of the instrument.

Monkey in the Garden

T to the 7th Power

Butch Robins

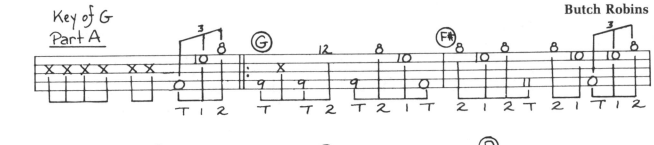

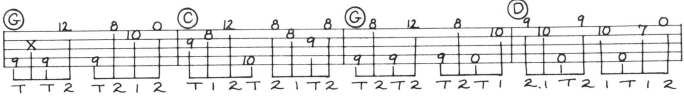

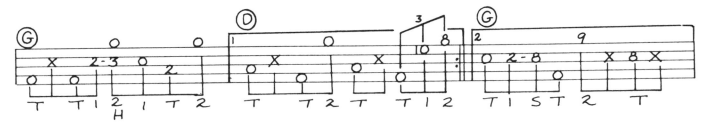

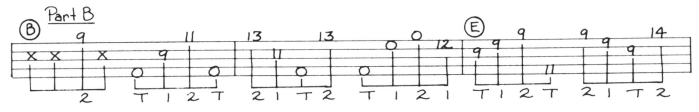

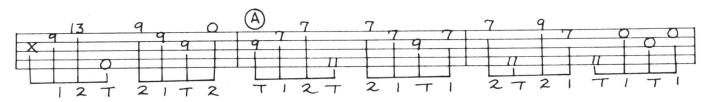

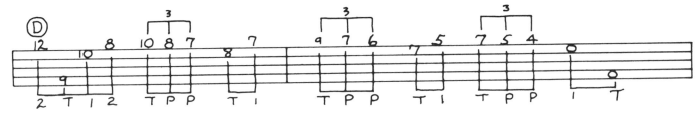

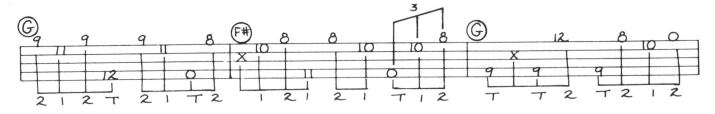

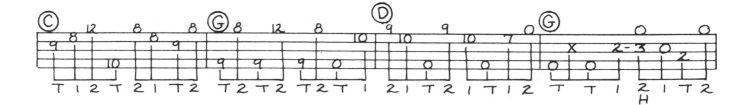

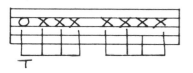

Poor Ellen Smith

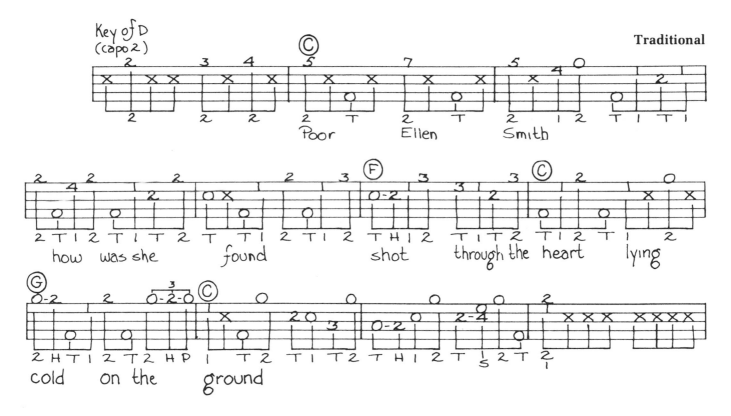

Larry McNeely

Larry McNeely with author.

I went to pick me up a banjo mute the other day and the guy behind the counter said, "Banjo mute? What kind of banjo do you play?" I said five string. He said, "Why do you want to mute the five string banjo?" There you have the example of the fixed idea of how banjo should be played and should stay that way. You know, don't change it. But if it doesn't change it's just going to lay there and it's been doing the same thing for lots of years now. Guys are wanting to do new things with it, like have more fun with it now. So the new ideas that are happening, that's where I'm taking it.

The interesting thing is that Larry hasn't been exposing his new ideas to appreciative bluegrass audiences, but rather to the frequenters of such places as Lake Tahoe, Reno, and Las Vegas.

That's a long way from Lafayette, Indiana, where Larry was born on January 3, 1948. He knew early on that he was going to be involved with music. Though he first got turned on to the banjo when he was thirteen, he didn't actually start playing until he was fifteen. A year later, he was on his way to Tennessee to live and pick with Charlie Collins (Roy Acuff's guitarist). "I'd come from Indiana and I was

supposed to finish up school. I think I was sixteen by the time I got to Charlie's house. That's why I didn't have to go back to school, and I said, 'I want to play, that's all I want to do.' So I got a job where I could practice on the job when there weren't customers in the shop, which was very nice for me. So I lived there and practiced every day."

From time to time, Larry would pop into Nashville to catch the Grand Ole Opry. On one of these occasions his talents were brought to the attention of Roy Acuff. "I was playing in the alley next to the Old Opry with Charlie Collins, and Mac Magaha, a fiddle player, heard us play and took us back to Roy's dressing room where we played a tune for him. Soon after that I moved to Nashville, got a job at Sho Bud, and Roy found me up there working one day and asked me if I'd like to go on tour, and that was how I started." Larry travelled with Acuff for almost three years, during which time "he taught me a lot about timing, and being on time, never being late for a gig, doing your best job."

In 1967, in the middle of his stint with Roy, Larry took a side trip to Chicago to demonstrate some instruments for the Dobro Company. It was there that he met Glen Campbell. "He was from Mosrite and I was from Dobro and we were in the same room and we kept crossing paths like that." The two played together, and the memory must have stuck with Glen, because in September 1969, he asked Larry to fill John Hartford's slot on his television show. Larry accepted, but in taking the job he got hooked up with a Hollywood manager.

> He disappointed me from playing the banjo by saying, "Since you're on network TV and a semi-star of the show, you ought to put out an album that would appeal to more people." And I was sick of writing all these banjo things. None of them ever got recorded. And he just kept saying, "Don't be identified with the banjo." My second album didn't have any banjo at all. That was late '70, '71. Then I got reenergized with the banjo. I started picking it up, playing it and having fun with it. Started moving on from that point.

This rekindling of Larry's banjo spark eventually led to his next job, with the Smothers Brothers. Herb Pederson, formerly of the Dillards, had been offered the spot, but declined it to do session work in L.A. Pederson suggested to Larry that he write a letter to Tommy Smothers. He did; but by the time he got an answer, he was already committed to a tour with Burl Ives. So Larry had to wait a year until the job came around again (in November 1975), at which point he took it.

Although it might seem frustrating for a bluegrass musician to play to audiences that don't know the difference between a flat pick and a fingerpick, Larry's travels to Nevada with Glen Campbell and the Smothers have given him a unique opportunity to place his banjo in less traditional musical settings. After all, it's unlikely that you would ever see Larry perform Beethoven's Fifth Symphony with a twenty-four piece orchestra at Bean Blossom. But at the Alladin's Club in Las Vegas, anything is possible. It's all a reflection of Larry's movement away from the standard bluegrass inputs as he looks to other sources for musical stimulation. "I listen to Chick Corea a whole lot. Some girl came over and brought us a tape by this guy playing some Eric Satie, which I'd never heard of, and I'm just thoroughly into him. I really listen to a lot of piano for some reason. I'm trying to expand the banjo so it doesn't have to play just bluegrass. It can be used for semi-classical stuff, rock'n' roll, easily."

Aside from music, one of Larry's most important involvements has been Scientology, a religion founded by L. Ron Hubbard.

> When a guy gets better through his training and processing, his byproducts become better. Like I wanted to be a better musician, and all that's occurring because I'm just making it happen.

> I'm not sitting back and letting it happen. So I wanted to become more cause than effect. Most people like to be a cause. I also found things that could help me write better and hold my attention. I wouldn't get involved in forty million other things. I wasn't ironing my clothes or washing the dishes. I was playing the banjo and I have a lot of fun with it. It had become so serious and I'm just not that serious. I like to sit back and enjoy myself. Because if I get too serious the audience is going to see this guy's really serious. We shouldn't have any gaiety about us because this guy's too into it. I just want to be happy about it, play the music, write. I can do all those things and expand. I'm totally into expansion of my abilities.

Style

While Larry's technical and creative abilities have long been legendary, the two songs included here demonstrate that he is also in the vanguard of the new experimental banjo scene.

"Zubenelgenubi" is based on an amazing stampede of chromatic triplets and is somewhat reminiscent of mosquito music. In short, you'll have to hear this one to believe it. Besides helping you to develop nimble fingers, this tune will make you more familiar with some of the new age positions on the neck. I find it hard to pick out individual elements here because the tune is conceived of more as a cohesive unit than as a series of licks. So simply listen, play, and enjoy.

"Rhapsody for Banjo" is more spacious than "Zubenelgenubi" (it contains four parts) and is equally impressive. Like "Zube," it's almost entirely melodic; in fact, it's devoid of Scruggs licks. In the past, only fiddle tunes were approached like this. But with "Rhapsody" and other examples of the new banjo music, there's less dependence on the familiar landmarks of Scruggs style. Compositional influences are no longer restricted to bluegrass, but now include a wide range of music: jazz, classical, and rock. This allows for more personalized expression, and often results in expanded musical conceptions. For instance, "Rhapsody" is comprised of four unified sections instead of two. To keep a common thread running throughout, Larry plays a descending C minor scale in the first five bars of *Part A* and then evenly distributes fragments of the scale among the other sections. This is similar to the Indian practice of brushing across the open strings of a sitar at the beginning of a raga to set the mode on which the rest of the raga will be based.

Speaking in more general terms, Larry's playing on both of these tunes is phenomenal—fast, clean, and coherent—and gives us all something to strive toward.

Zubenelgenubi

Larry McNeely

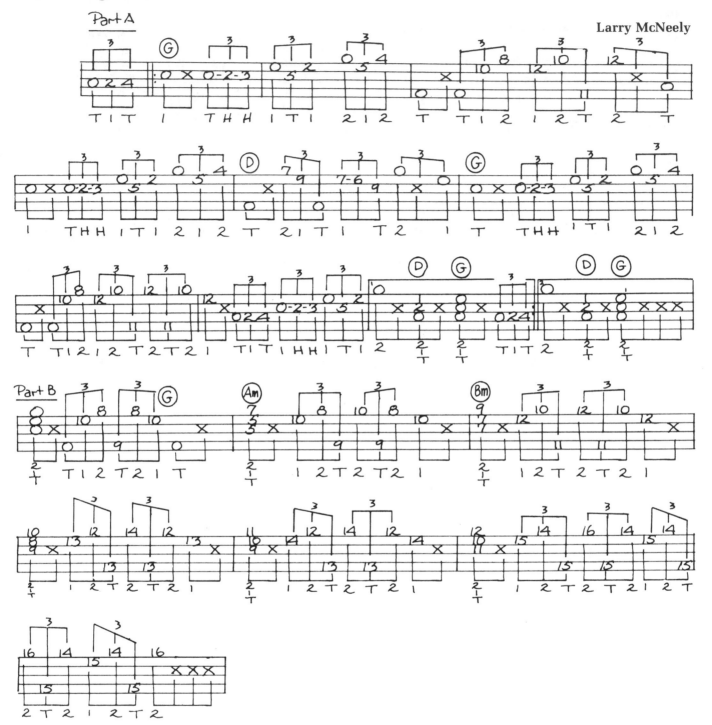

Rhapsody for Banjo #1 (Juarez)

Larry McNeely

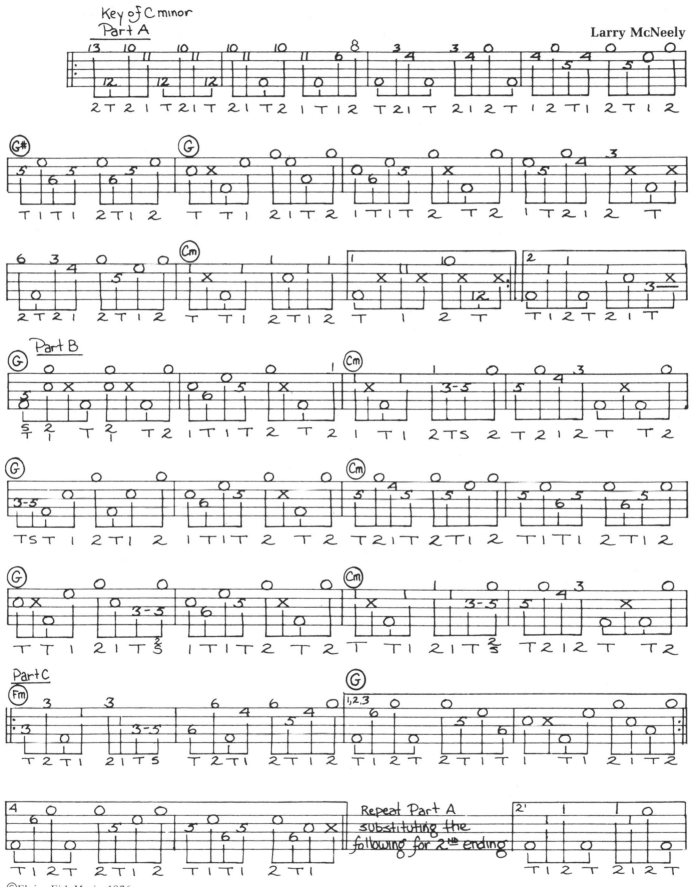

71

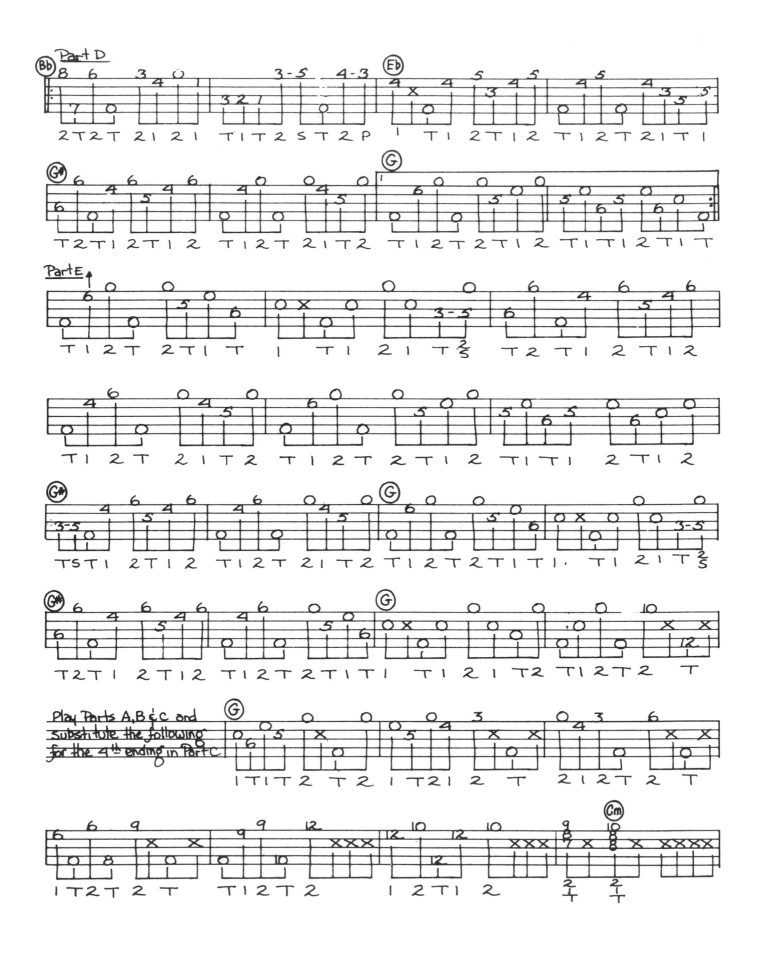

Pat Cloud

Pat Cloud (L) and Bill Knopf (a fine California picker and author) chewing on the strings.

Pat Cloud is an elusive figure. Though some people know of him only by rumor, he is, in fact, alive, well, and playing locally in southern California. Indeed, he is one of the most strikingly original banjo players around. He combines bebop jazz lines with fiddle tunes, Django Reinhardt with Earl Scruggs, and places the entire mixture in a melodic flow that just won't quit.

Aside from being a mind-boggling player, Pat is very articulate about what he's doing, as the following interview demonstrates.

TONY: *How did you get started?*
PAT: *I got into banjo because there was one on my wall at my stepfather's house. I picked it up and played it with a pick for about three months with three strings on her until somebody told me to get two more strings and use fingers. I was listening to Flatt and Scruggs records. I learned all of the Foggy Mountain Banjo album, started listening to fiddle tunes, I went to a lot of fiddler's conventions, a lot of things from Byron Berline. Started listening to old 78s of ragtime piano, swing, Bix Beiderbeck, Coleman Hawkins, Django Reinhardt, Benny Goodman, the boppers, and then wherever it's at today.*
T: *How did you get into doing scales and jazz chord substitutions?*
P: *I just wanted to play banjo differently because I was getting bored by playing the same. I*

was not getting bored by the style. I like the music a lot, but you like different things to play. Music sort of overlaps and is adaptable in context.
T: *Why haven't people played jazz on the banjo yet? Do you think there are limitations of the banjo that prevent people from doing that?*
P: *It doesn't have eight octaves like the guitar or piano.*
T: *What would you suggest playing to get into some of the stuff you're doing?*
P: *Oh, learn all your major scales and learn all your minor scales. That includes harmonic, melodic, and natural. Every chord change can be painted by a scale. In bluegrass, I'll say one or two scales, in jazz, three or four.*
T: *You do so much practicing—two and three hours a day.*
P: *That's not true. I don't practice enough, actually. I'm lucky if I get away with four. I don't think it's easy to do at once. You have to work up to it. You have to really feel it's worth it. If you don't feel your practicing is going to do any good, you aren't inspired. It's also a matter of getting over the trauma of sounding rotten. As Richard Greene once said, "You just have to play and sound rotten until you get the hang of it; not to be afraid and traumatic, and fall on your face a bunch of times."*
T: *Do you have any other thoughts on breaking out of old patterns on the banjo?*
P: *We all have finger habits, and getting your*

hand in tune with your ear is the big trip. You hear a note way up there, you should try to hit it. Putting it on the spot where you want it. A lot of busy work. I'm not nearly as dedicated as I plan to become.

Style

Breaking with all tradition, Pat Cloud has managed to create a jazzy and expansive style that owes very little to bluegrass, but a lot to the intricacies of music theory. He *can* play the Scruggs licks and fiddle tunes ("Allen's Hornpipe" demonstrates this). But when it comes to improvising off a song like "Nine Pound Hammer," he approaches it as a jazzman would.

To do this, Pat has spent many hours practicing scale exercises and poring over books on jazz theory. The knowledge gained from doing this has made him more conscious of what he's playing. Instead of running through a series of licks automatically, he thinks as he picks. This has given him access to a whole universe of new sounds, some of which are found in the two variations of "Nine-Pound Hammer."

The key to these breaks is Pat's use of substitutions—a term that refers, in this case, to scales which replace the ones normally associated with particular chords. For instance, instead of playing a G scale against the G chord in the first three bars of the first variation, Pat employs notes from this blues scale (some of the notes are an octave higher than they appear here):

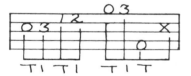

Similarly, the first bar in C consists of an F scale (minus a few notes) painted against the C or C7 chord. The resulting sound works because the same notes found in an F scale also occur in a C7 scale. The following F scale begins with two leading notes and contains, within the two bar lines, the first eight notes Pat plays against the C chord.

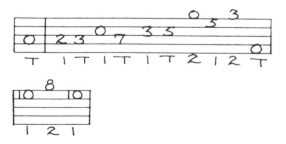

The D lick is simply based on a D7 chord, with the addition of the fourth note in the bar as a chromatic

lead-in to the seventh interval of the scale. This will be a good one to add to your collection.

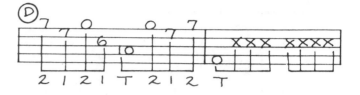

The first three measures of the second variation are based on the following D minor scale:

Once you realize that a D minor sounds good with a G, you can do a little transposing and discover that an A minor scale works with a D, a G minor scale with a C, and so on. That's the beauty of this whole thing. A little theory goes a long way. Take the C chord, for instance. Like the C chord in the first variation, this one is also colored by an F scale. By expanding on this knowledge, you'll find that you can play a G scale against a D chord, a C scale against a G chord, and on from there. Hopefully, some of these ideas will give you the incentive to experiment on your own.

One other thing you should notice is Pat's use of slides to facilitate movement from one note to another. This technique is underused in the melodic playing of most bluegrassers. This may be because slides as used here, produce more of a swing feel than might be considered appropriate in a traditional fiddle tune. At any rate, it's something to take into consideration.

"Allen's Hornpipe" (also known as "Alfie's Hornpipe") is based on the playing of the fine northwestern fiddler, Joe Pancerzewski, who in turn learned it from Alfie Myers of Edmonton, Alberta. Notice that the tune is dappled with triplets, a characteristic of the sprightly Canadian fiddle sound. The thing to watch out for here is the right-hand fingering. In several places, Pat crosses his thumb over his index finger. This may be unorthodox, but if Pat hears a particular sound that can't be conveniently produced by the right hand, he'll play it any way he can rather than avoid the notes. That's the point—we shouldn't be afraid to expand our musical boundaries. What at first may seem awkward, or even incomprehensible, can become second nature with applied knowledge and practice. Pat's music is a vivid example of this belief.

Nine Pound Hammer

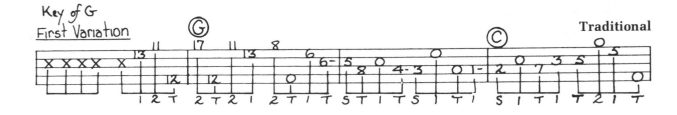

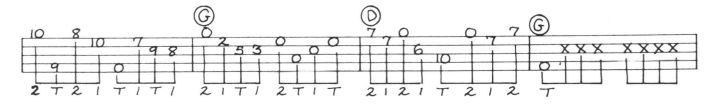

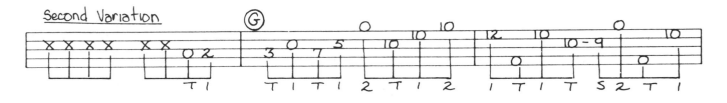

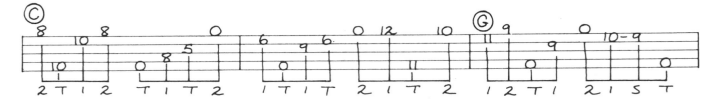

Allen's Hornpipe

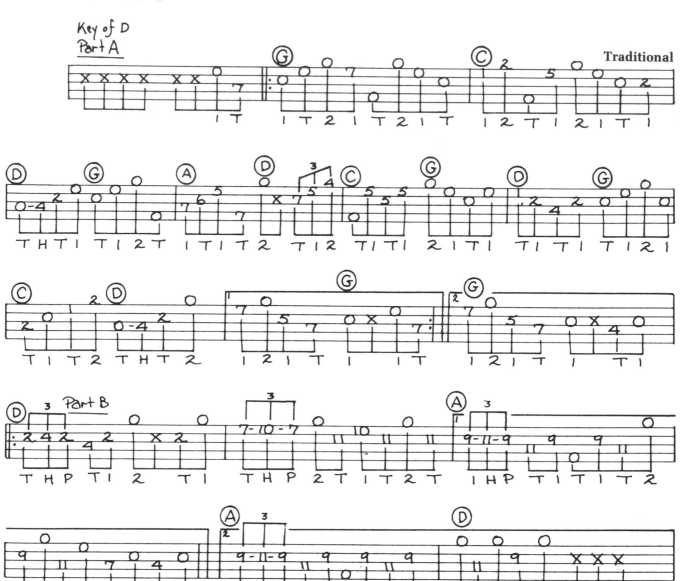

76

Fiddle Tunes

For a number of reasons, I found myself gravitating to fiddle tunes when the time came to choose material for this book. I was primarily attracted by the long-standing tradition that has kept these tunes in circulation throughout the years—the oral process that transmitted them from fiddler to fiddler, from generation to generation and in some cases, from country to country (most commonly from the British Isles to the United States).

A good number of these tunes are rooted in the Appalachians and go back quite a way. "Richmond Cotillion," for example, was played at Thomas Jefferson's inaugural ball. In many ways, the aging process has refined these tunes into miniature works of art; each one is perfect as it is. Within this perfection, though, there's room for variation; but only so long as the variant is "right." And what is right? As a fine fiddler once told me, "To actualize the old-time fiddle sound, never lose sight of the melody. You can improvise, but only within the boundaries of the melody." To make sure I was approaching that sound with accuracy, I adapted most of these tunes directly from the playing of the above-mentioned fiddler, Alan Kaufman (who has a book published by Oak, *Beginning Old Time Fiddle*). I came as close as I could to playing the songs note for note as he did. When that was inconvenient due to the differences between fiddle and banjo technique, I came up with my own variations.

Although Scruggs style can be helpful in approximating the sound of a fiddle tune, the melodic style allows you to get amazingly close to the literal melody. Bobby Thompson was really first to work with this approach. He put together a melodic version of "Arkansas Traveler" in 1957. Unfortunately, Bobby was ahead of his time; because of audience indifference, he was forced to shelve the fiddle tunes in favor of "Foggy Mountain Breakdown," and other grabbers of that ilk. Bill Keith met with considerably less public resistance. He got his versions of "Devil's Dream" and "Sailor's Hornpipe" out to the more accepting urban banjo players, and by 1964 melodics were spreading like kudzu.

If you haven't worked out much of this style before, this section will give you a chance to splash around a bit. These tunes will loosen up your right hand with new finger patterns, and your left hand with fresh positions on the fretboard.

Most important, these songs should forever dispel the notion that all fiddle tunes sound the same. It's true that when you're listening casually to a number of fiddle tunes in a row, especially if you're hearing them for the first time, the subtle nuances may pass you by. But here you have a chance to get right inside them. By playing them for a while, you'll experience the unique personality that each one possesses.

With this said, dive in.

Leather Britches

Traditional
Arranged by Bela Fleck

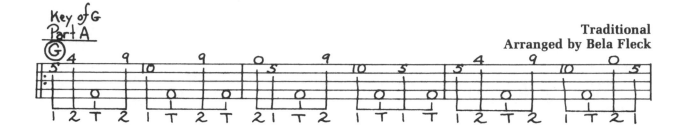

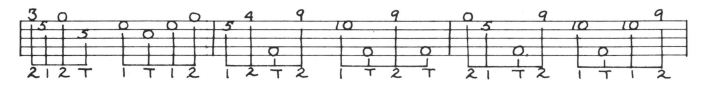

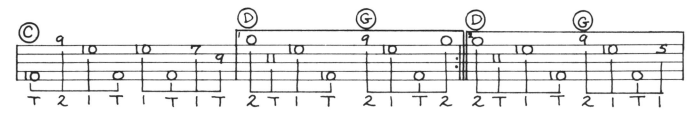

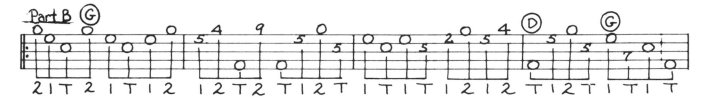

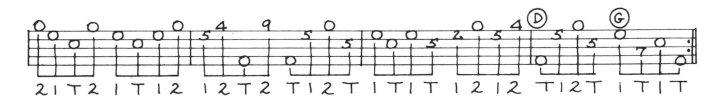

Hogeye

Traditional
Arranged by Tony Trischka and Alan Kaufman

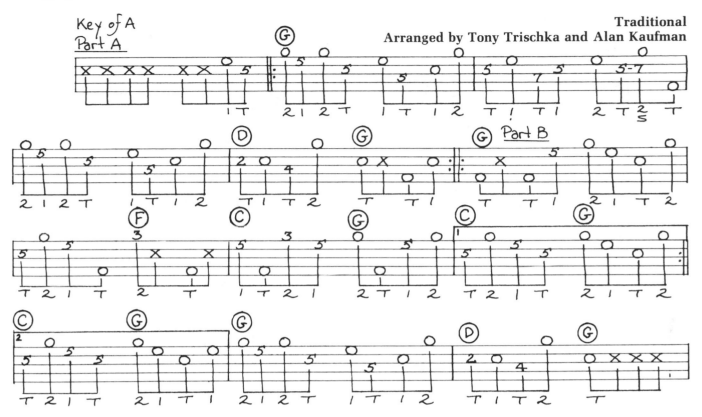

Cluck Old Hen

Traditional
Arranged by Tony Trischka

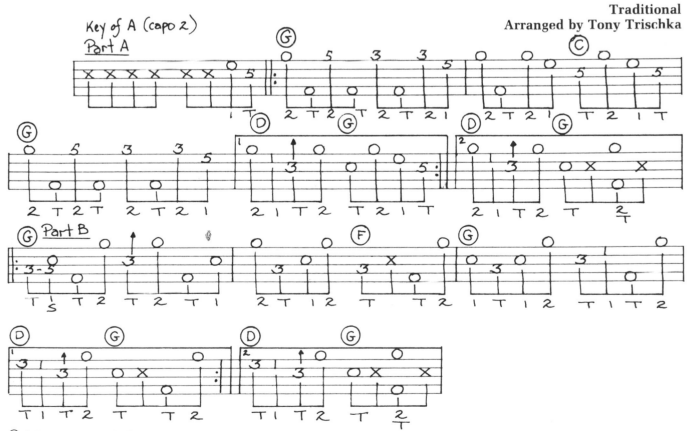

Old Joe Clark

Traditional
Arranged by Tony Trischka

Key of A (capo 2)
Part A

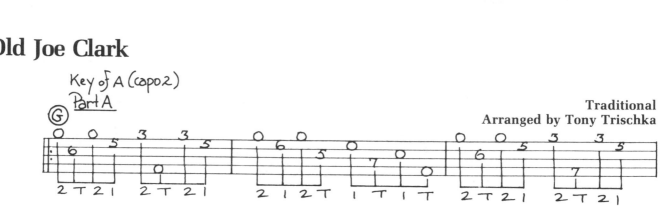

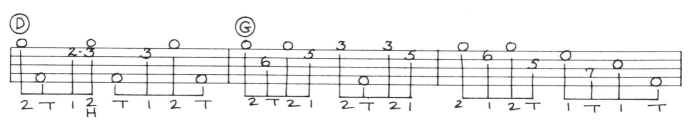

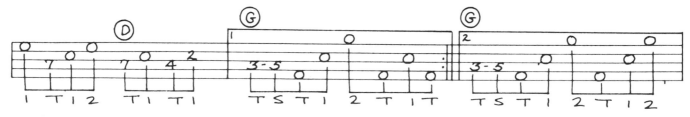

Part B

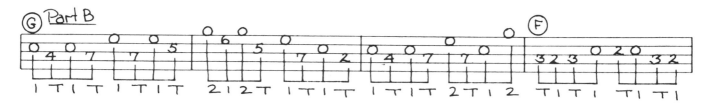

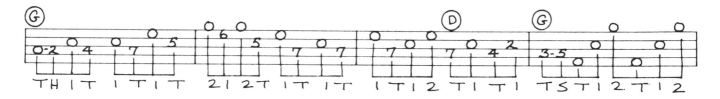

Mississippi Sawyer

Traditional
Arranged by Tony Trischka and Alan Kaufman

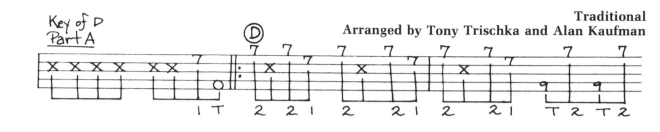

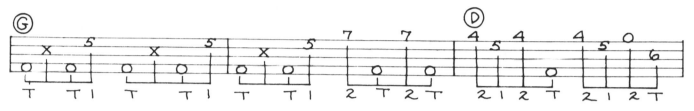

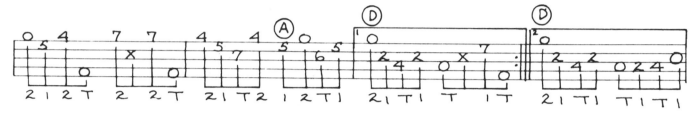

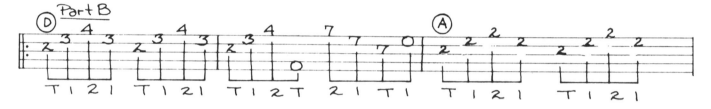

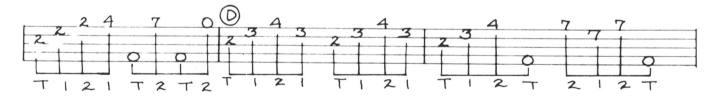

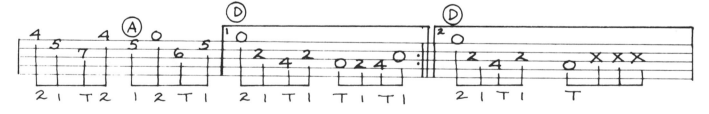

Cripple Creek

Traditional
Arranged by Tony Trischka

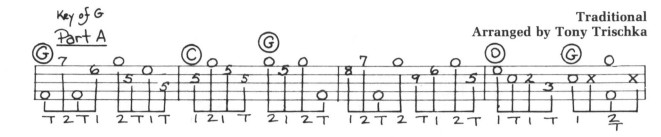

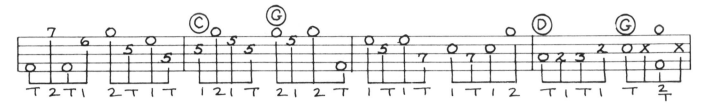

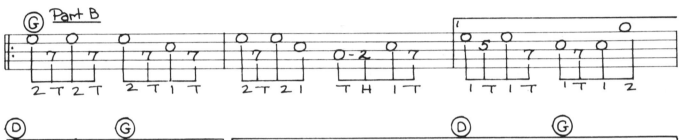

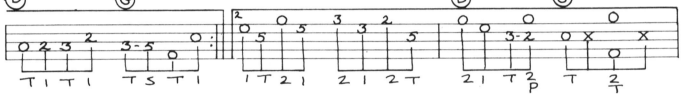

Growling Old Man and Woman

Traditional
Arranged by Bela Fleck

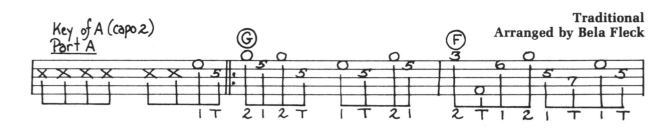

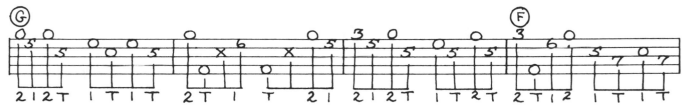

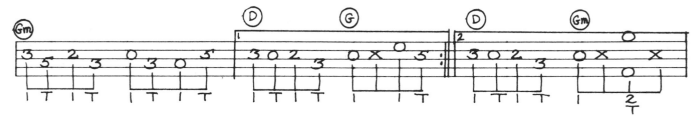

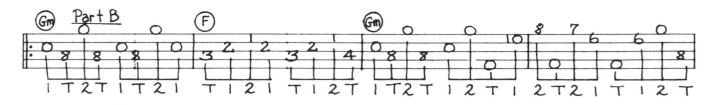

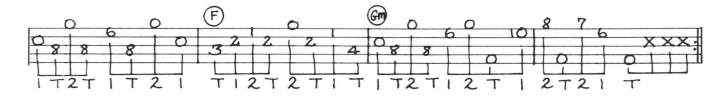

Sally Ann

Traditional
Arranged by Tony Trischka

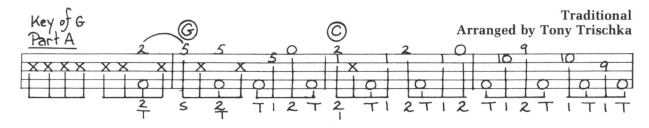

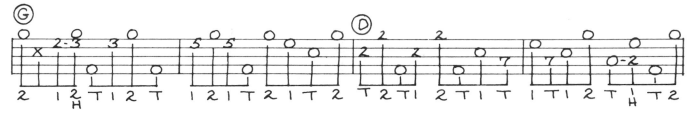

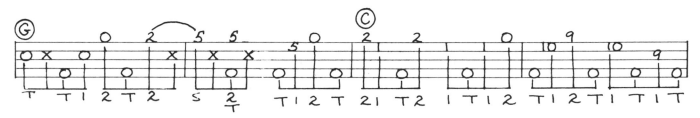

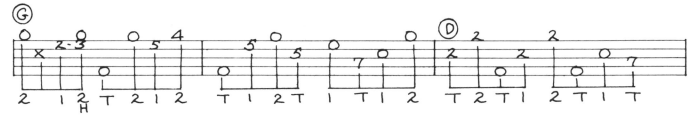

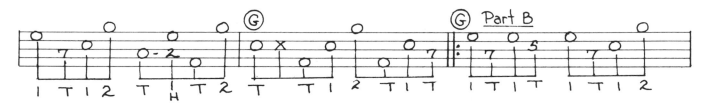

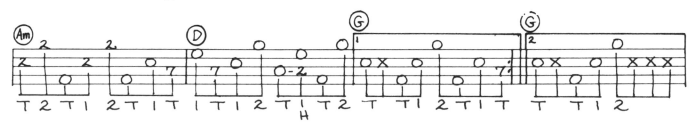

Kitchen Girl

Traditional
Arranged by Tony Trischka

Key of A
Part A

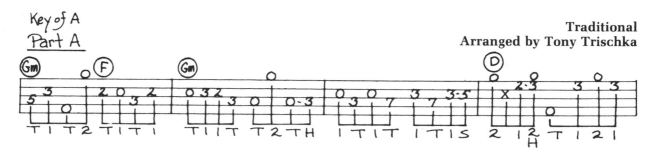

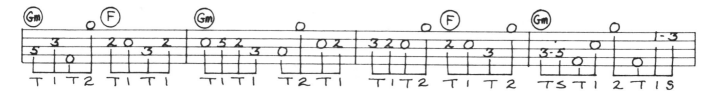

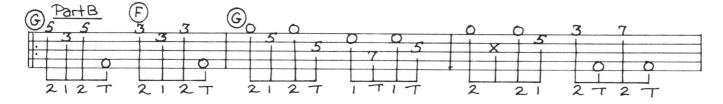

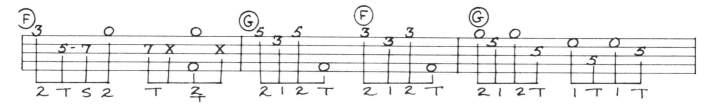

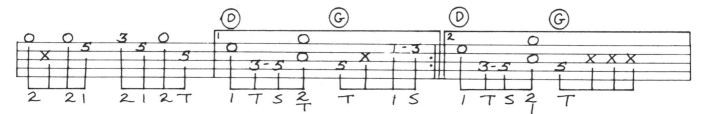

Green Willis

Traditional
Arranged by Tony Trischka and Alan Kaufman

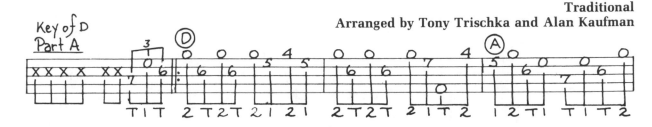

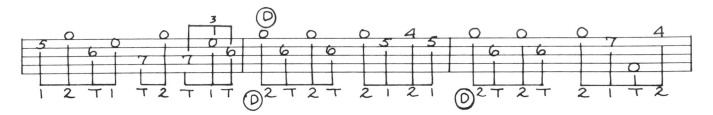

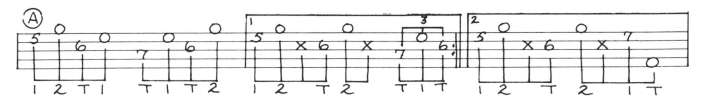

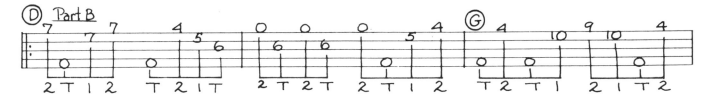

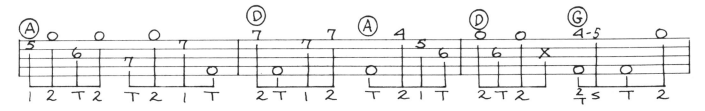

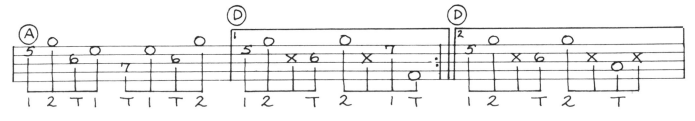

Hell Among the Yearlings

Traditional
Arranged by Tony Trischka

Key of G
Part A

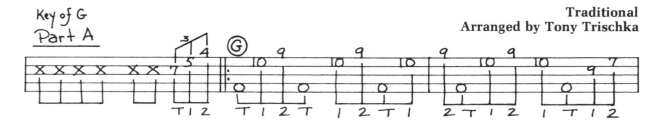

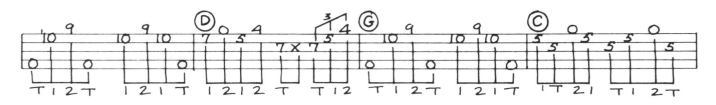

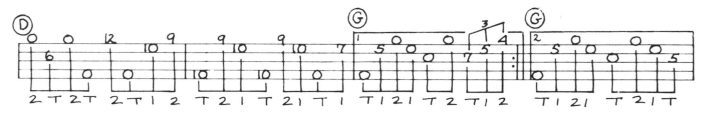

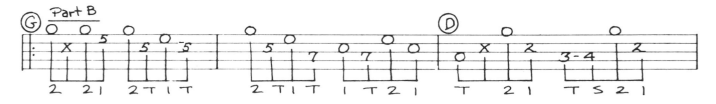

Part B

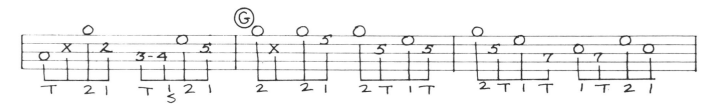

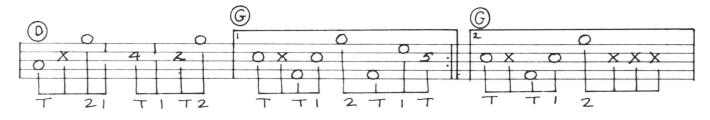

St. Anne's Reel

Traditional
Arranged by Bela Fleck

Key of D (capo 2)

Part A

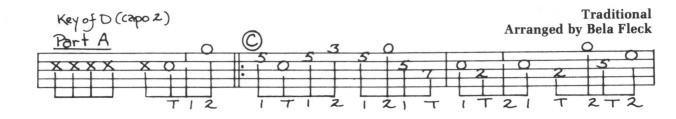

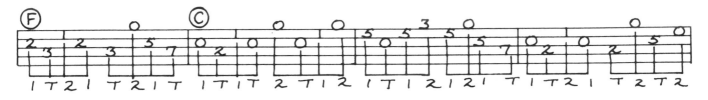

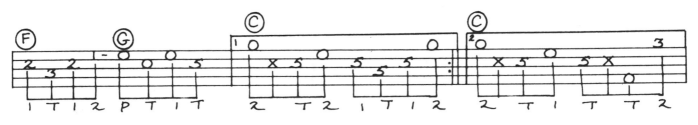

Part B

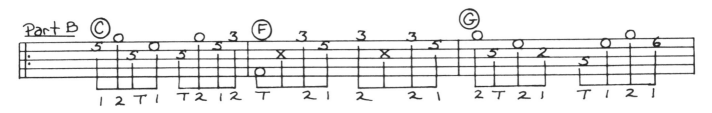

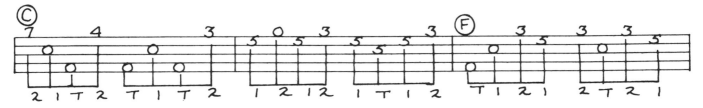

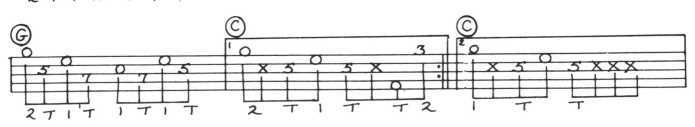

Richmond Cotillion

Traditional
Arranged by Tony Trischka

Key of D
(GCGBD – capo 2)
Part A

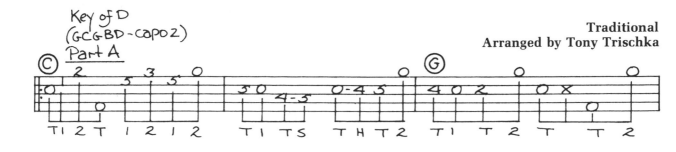

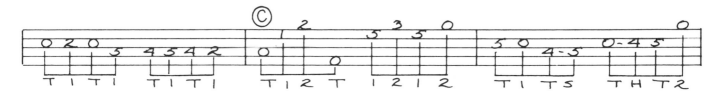

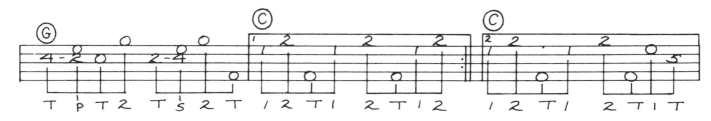

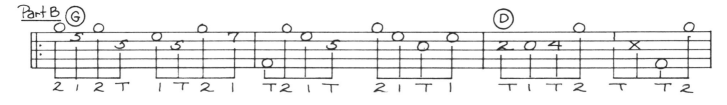

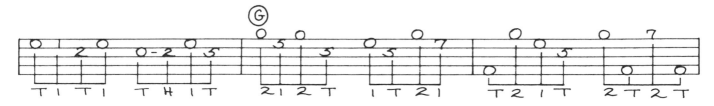

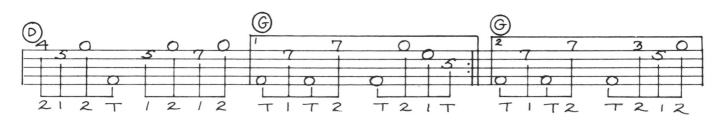

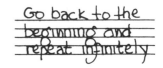

Go back to the beginning and repeat infinitely

Salt River

Key of A (capo 2)
Part A

Traditional
Arranged by Tony Trischka

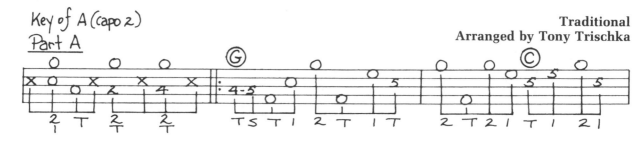

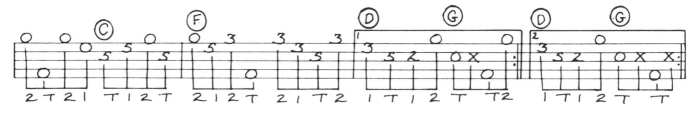

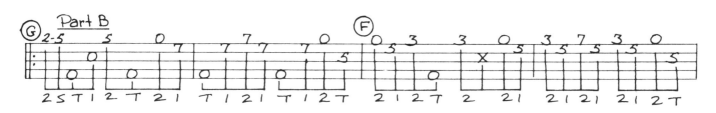

Part B

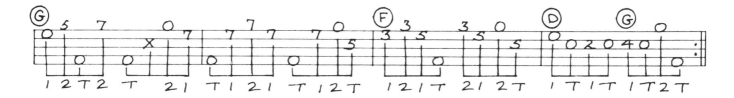

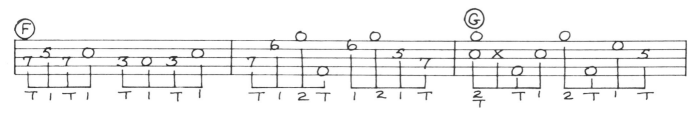

Elzic's Farewell

Traditional
Arranged by Tony Trischka and Alan Kaufman

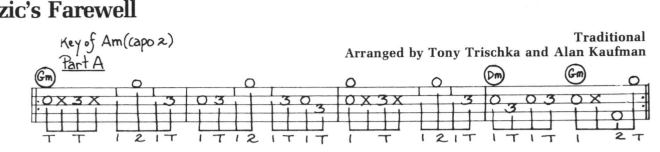

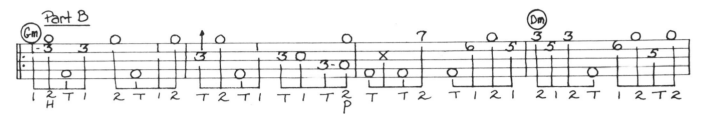

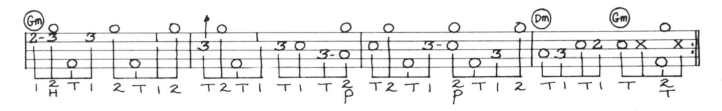

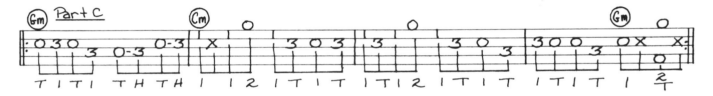

Forked Deer

Traditional
Arranged by Tony Trischka and Alan Kaufman

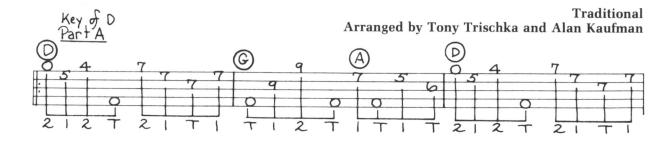

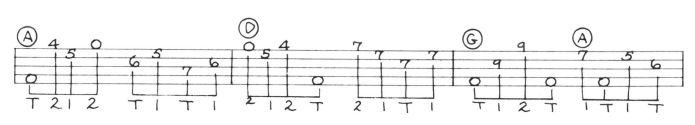

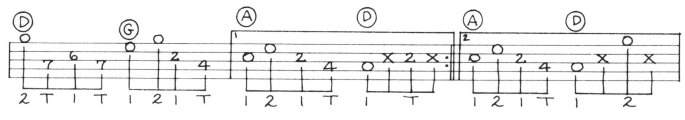

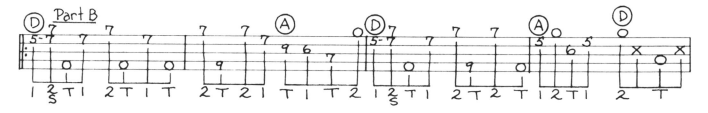

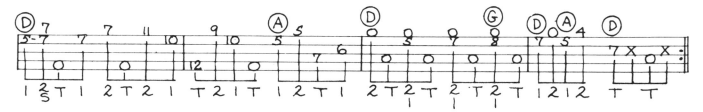

Whiskey Before Breakfast

Traditional
Arranged by Bela Fleck

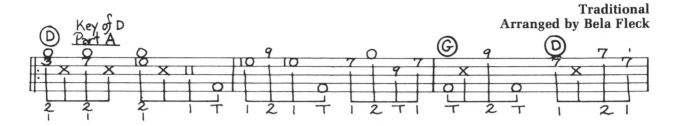

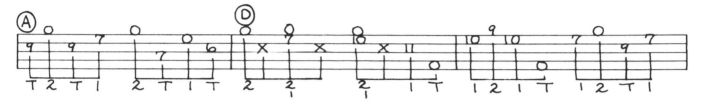

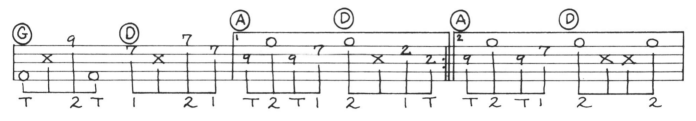

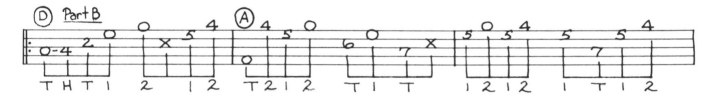

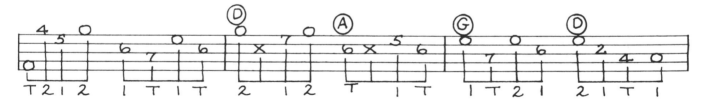

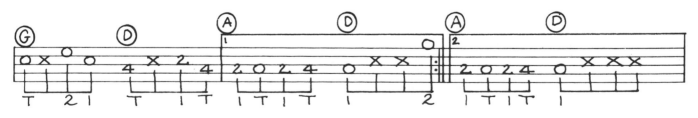

Kingston Springs

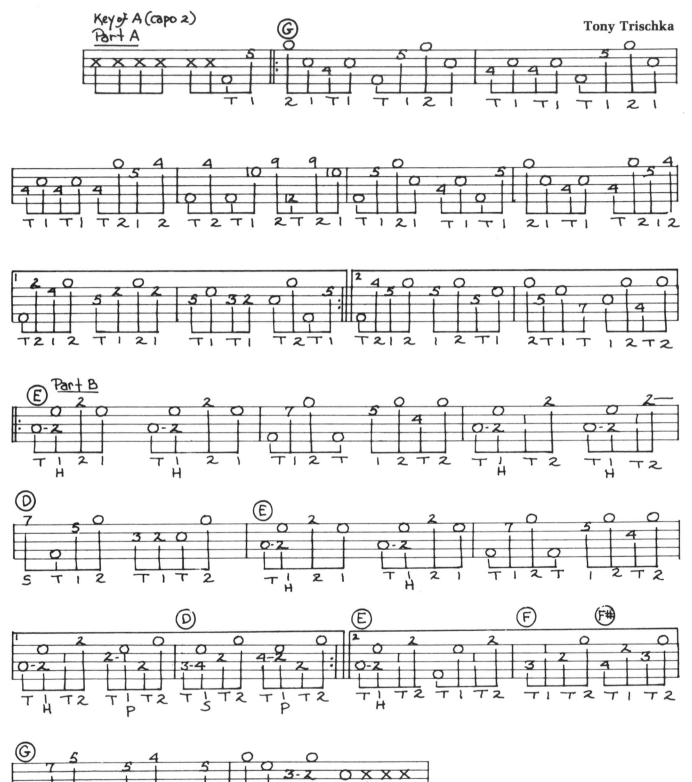

From Banjoland, Rounder Records 0087

Irish Washerwoman

Traditional
Arranged by Tony Trischka

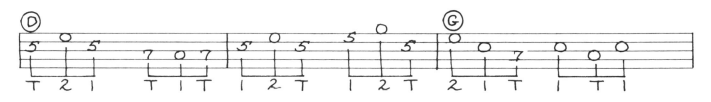

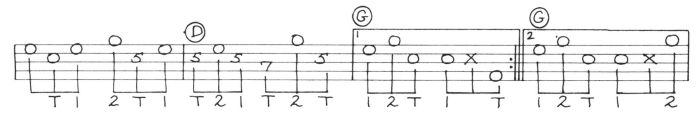

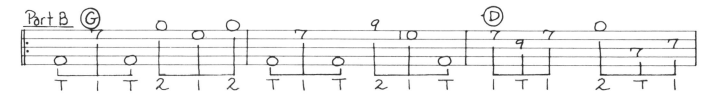

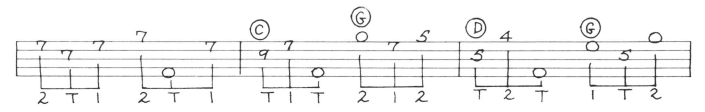

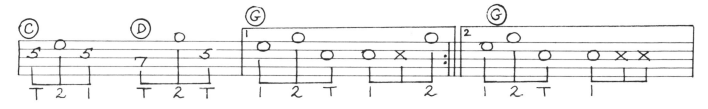

Cuckoo's Nest

Key of D (F#DGBD)

Part A

Traditional
Arranged by Tony Trischka

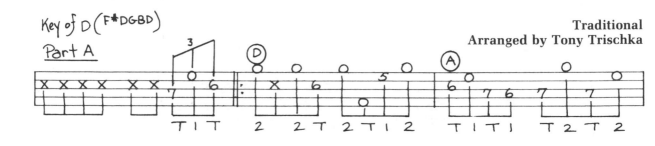

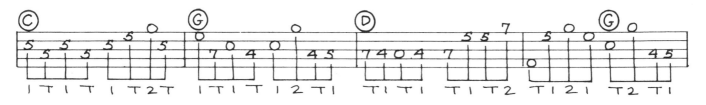

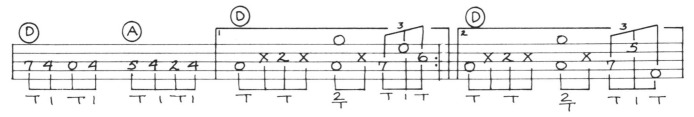

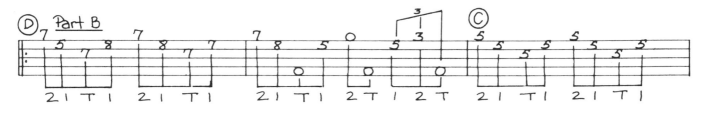

Part B

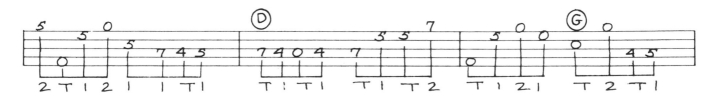

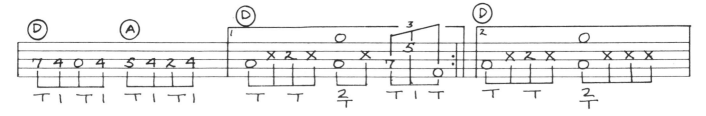

Black Mountain Rag

Traditional
Arranged by Tony Trischka

© Oak Publications, 1977

97

Bonaparte's Retreat

Traditional
Arranged by Tony Trischka

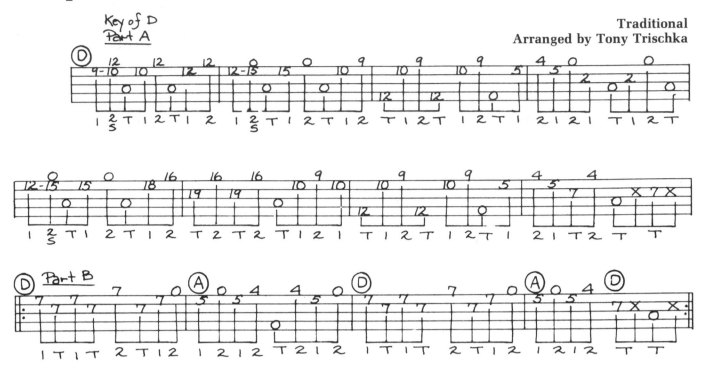

Galway Hornpipe

Traditional
Arranged by Tony Trischka and Hank Sapoznik

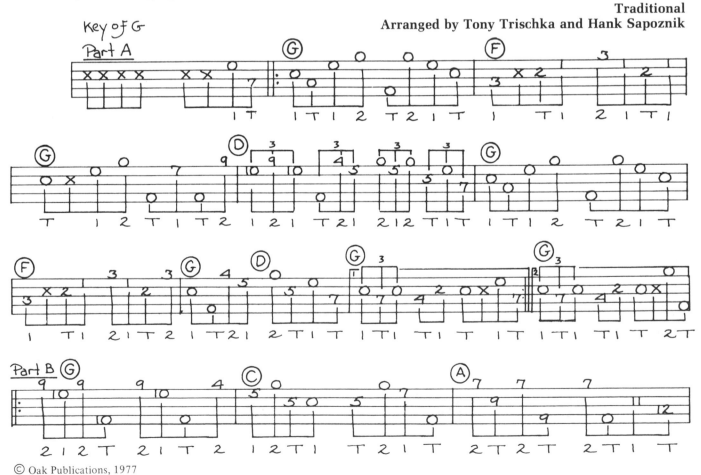

John Hickman—an excellent California banjoist and recent graduate of Byron Berline's *Sundance.*

Classic Sojourn

This section features one classic banjo tune (Vess Ossman's "Yankee Doodle") and three "serious" classical works adapted to the banjo.

By today's standards "Yankee Doodle" is a bit trite, but it did provide a good improvisatory vehicle for banjoists at the turn of the century; this version is actually quite charming. It's characterized by a half-time, two-finger *A* part and a three-finger, chordally textured *B* part. Although this is essentially a note-for-note transcription from the original Ossman 78, I did make some adjustments in the left and right hand fingerings to help the flow. In the classic style, for instance, the longer runs (line three measure three, and line five measure five) are generally played on a single string. Without a lot of practice, though, it's impossible to execute this fingering cleanly. So I've distributed the notes over several strings in order to achieve economy of movement. Classic banjo technique also dictates that runs on the first string be played with the first and second fingers of the right hand. This is by no means an impossible feat, but I've opted for the thumb and index finger in order to keep things more within a bluegrass framework.

The three remaining tunes are adaptations of classical pieces by Beethoven, Paganini and Bach. The Beethoven and Paganini pieces are particularly satisfying because they adapt so well to the banjo. In fact, if you play the Beethoven with a bit of a lilt, it will sound almost like a fiddle tune.

The Paganini also adapts nicely to the banjo. The *B* part features a beautiful melodic flow and fluid chord changes to match. In case you're confused by the Ddm indication at the beginning of the fourth line, it indicates a diminished D chord (see Appendix 1 for further information):

Ddim.

Bach's "Two Part Invention" is more of an undertaking. It requires two banjos and a good sense of space. (You'll notice several measures where only one note is being played.) Since this piece is probably the most challenging in the book, you should listen to it first on record. Get a feel for what's going on before sitting down with your instrument. Although this "Invention" is performed in C on the piano, it appears here in the key of G to accommodate the range of the banjo. Keep in mind that the top banjo line represents the right hand on the piano, and the lower line the left hand. While I've only had a chance to play this piece a few times as a duet, I can tell you the results are really satisfying, so keep at it.

Hopefully this section will inspire you to make your own classical adaptations for banjo. It will help if you can read music, but if not, adapt by ear. You'll find yourself using bluegrass techniques—especially the melodic style—but the melodies will be fresh and should give you a new perspective on the kinds of sounds you can get out of your instrument.

Yankee Doodle

Key of C (GCGBD)

Part A

Traditional

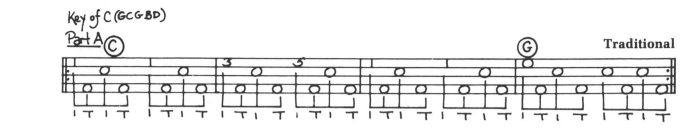

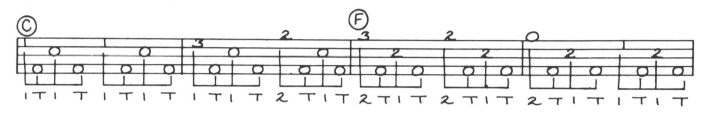

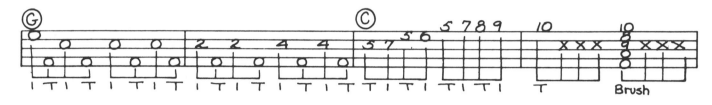

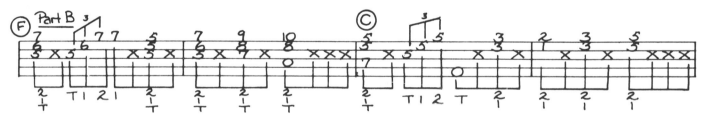

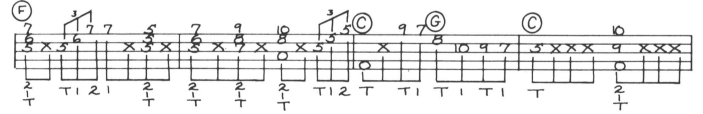

From Banjoland, Rounder Records 0087

101

Beethoven Mandolin Sonata in C Major

Traditional
Arranged by Tony Trischka and Hank Sapoznik

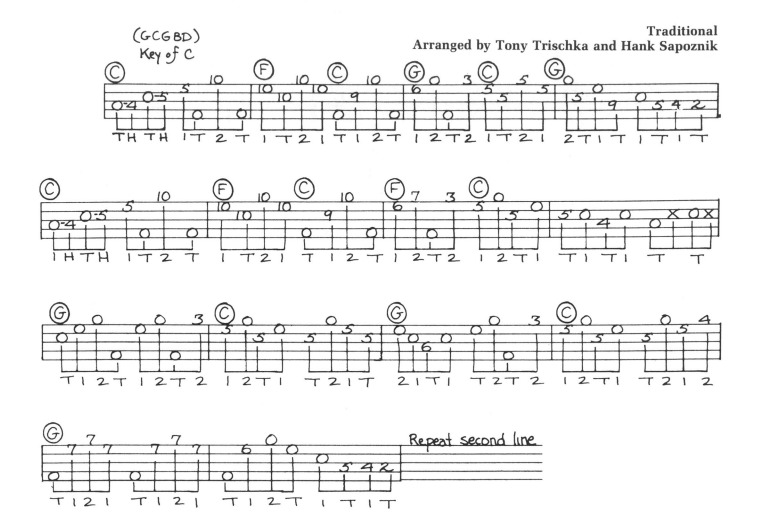

Paganini Violin Caprice #24

Traditional
Arranged by Tony Trischka and Barry Mitterhoff

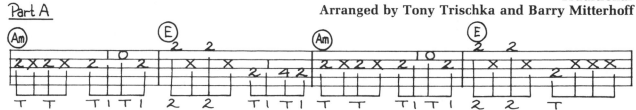

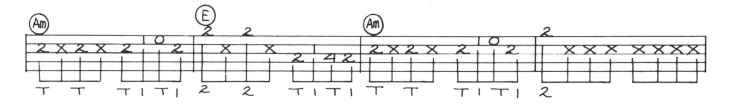

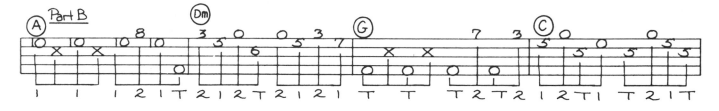

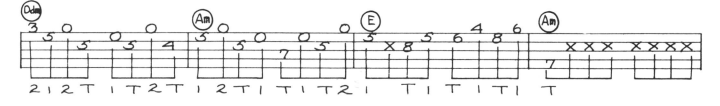

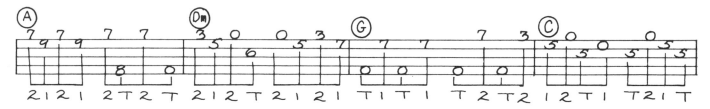

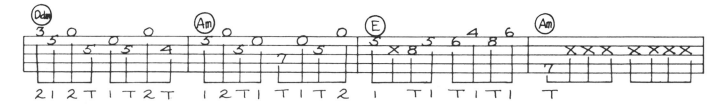

Bach Two Part Invention #1

Arranged by Bela Fleck and Evan Stover

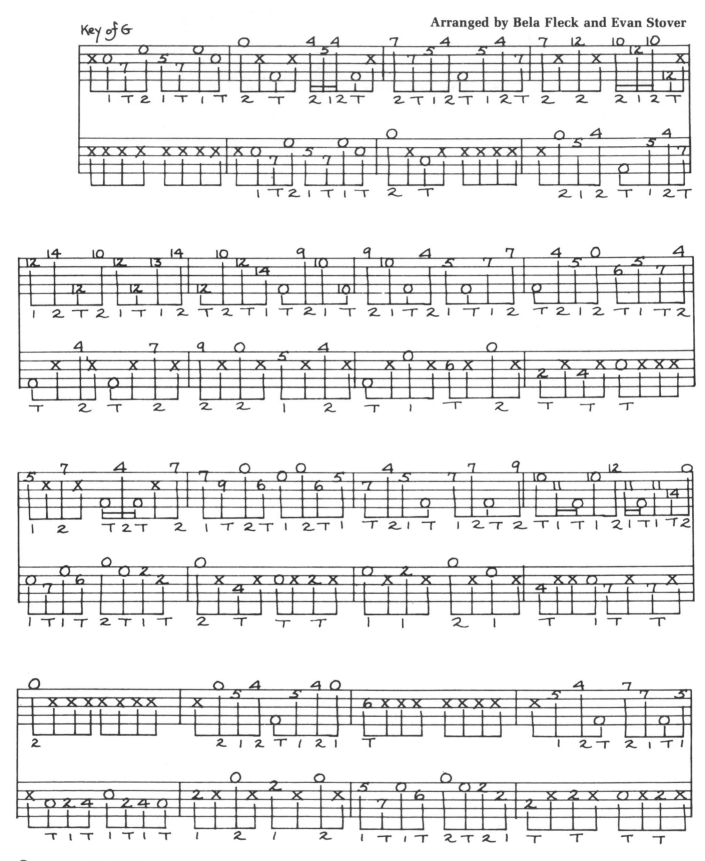

104

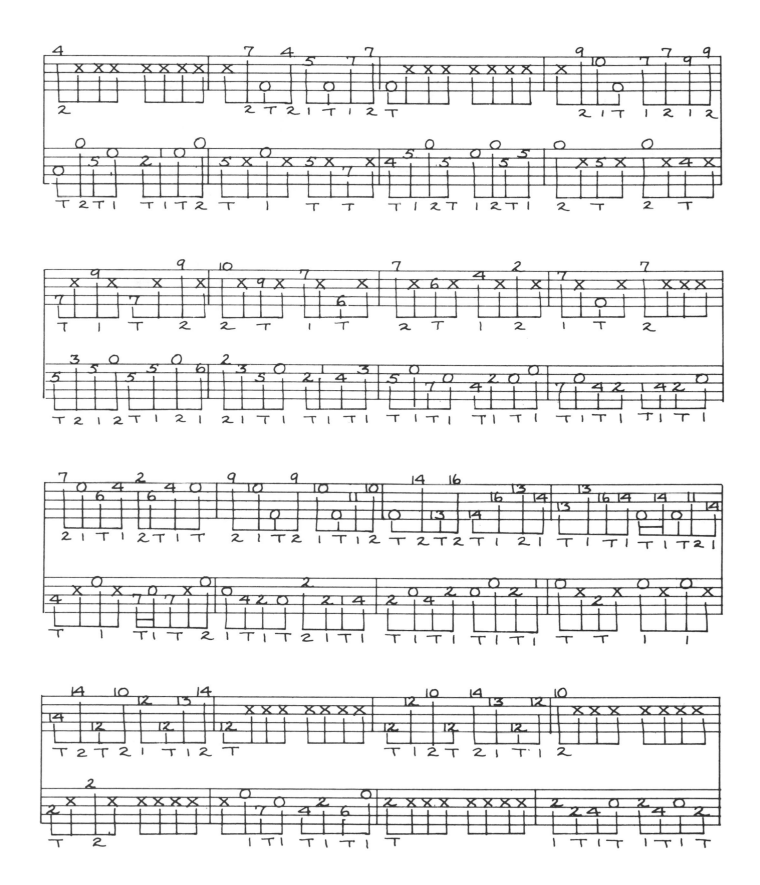

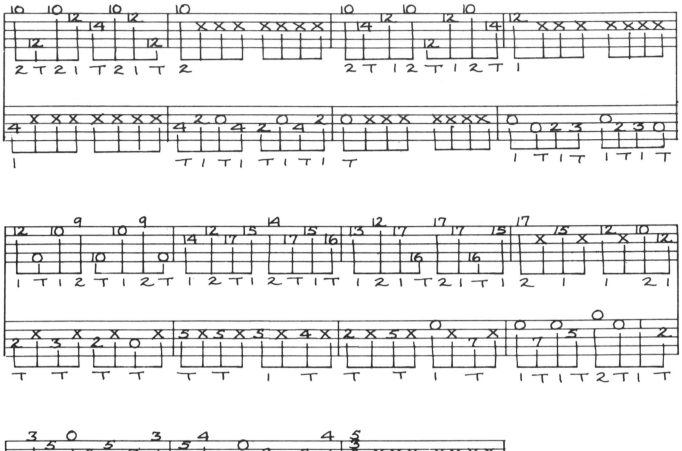

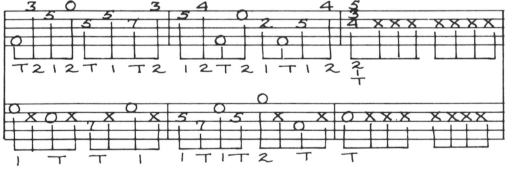

Bonus Bluegrass Section

You are now entering the bonus bluegrass section. This is a cavalcade of tunes, songs, blues, and rags which in one way or another fall under the general heading of bluegrass. This is popular material that you'll be able to put to practical use in your jam sessions or gigs. I've tried to make these breaks as middle of the road as possible so that you can play them on stage without being accused of going too far by the traditionalists, or not far enough by the modernists. Mind you, they're not muzak; just straight-ahead bluegrass. Also, keep in mind that these breaks are intended to trigger your own improvisations rather than be *the* way to play a particular song. Work them up and learn from them. Then go on from there, adding your own licks and rolls.

Finally, I would like to note that these are my own arrangements, with the exception of Carl Jackson's "Orange Blosson Special" Bill Emerson's "Sweet Dixie," Alan Munde's "New River Train," and Peter Wernick's "Blueberry Ripple."

Bela Fleck (currently working with Boston based *Tasty Licks*) is an amazing young player whose exploits in the outer reaches of banjo thought and technique place him on the crest of the wave of the future.

Alan Munde

Bill Emerson, 1972.

107

Train 45

Traditional
Arranged by Tony Trischka

Shady Grove

Traditional
Arranged by Tony Trischka

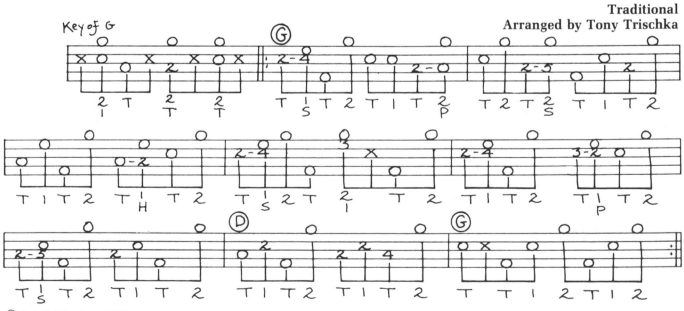

Roll in My Sweet Baby's Arms

Traditional
Arranged by Tony Trischka

Ruben's Train

Traditional
Arranged by Tony Trischka

(F#D F#AD)
Key of D

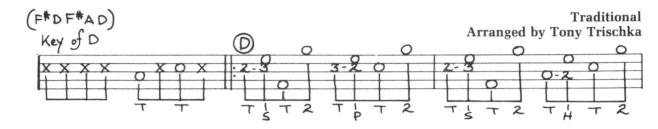

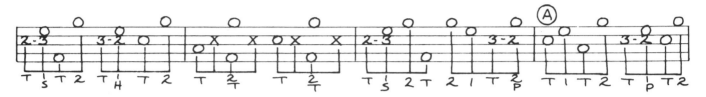

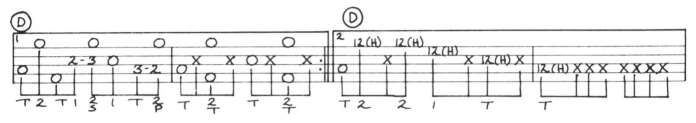

D Melodic Variation

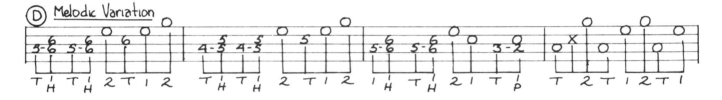

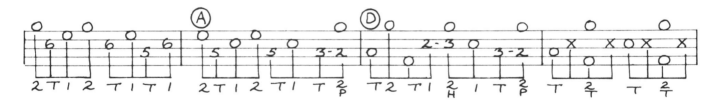

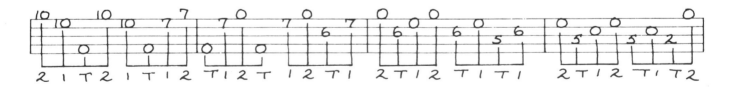

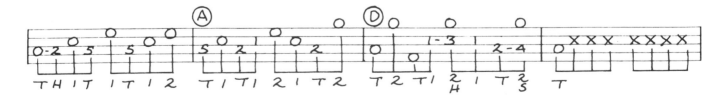

Little Darlin' Pal of Mine

Traditional
Arranged by Tony Trischka

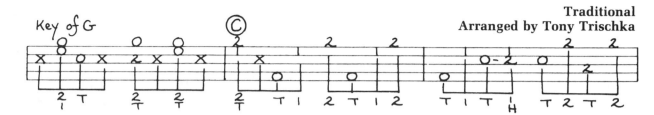

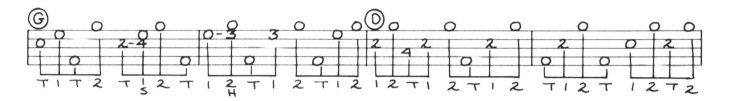

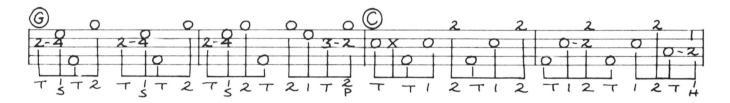

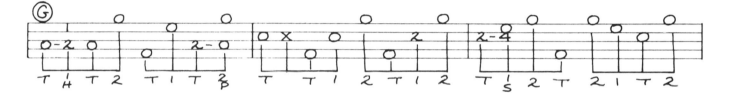

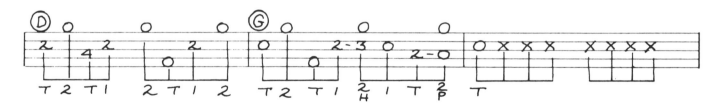

John Henry

Traditional
Arranged by Tony Trischka

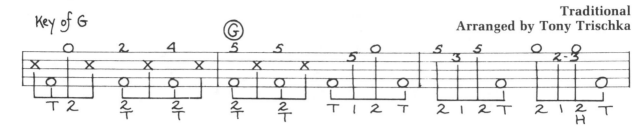

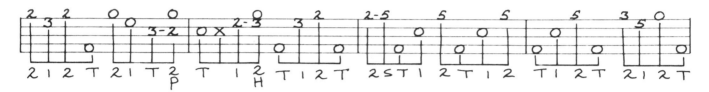

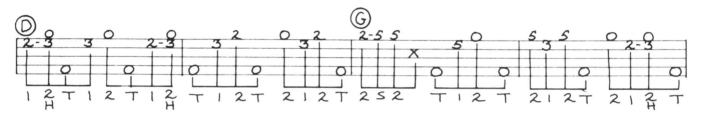

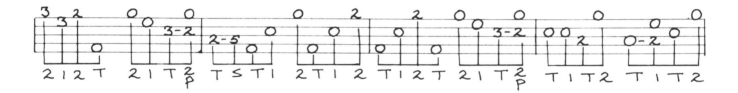

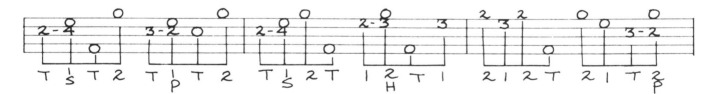

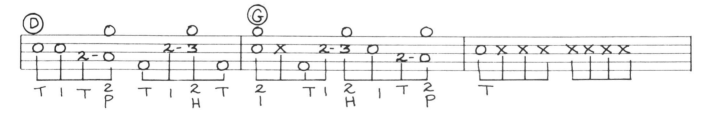

Salty Dog

Traditional
Arranged by Tony Trischka

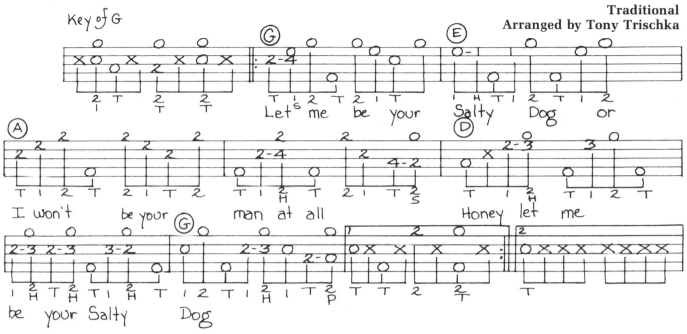

Swing Low Sweet Chariot

Traditional
Arranged by Tony Trischka

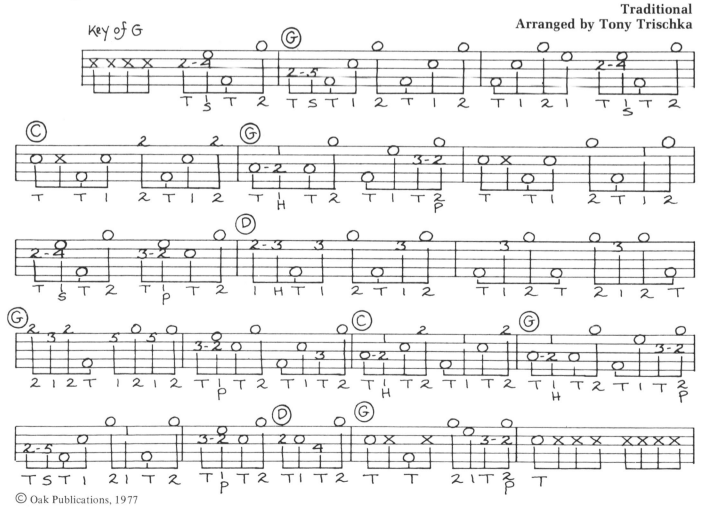

Sitting on Top of the World

Traditional
Arranged by Tony Trischka

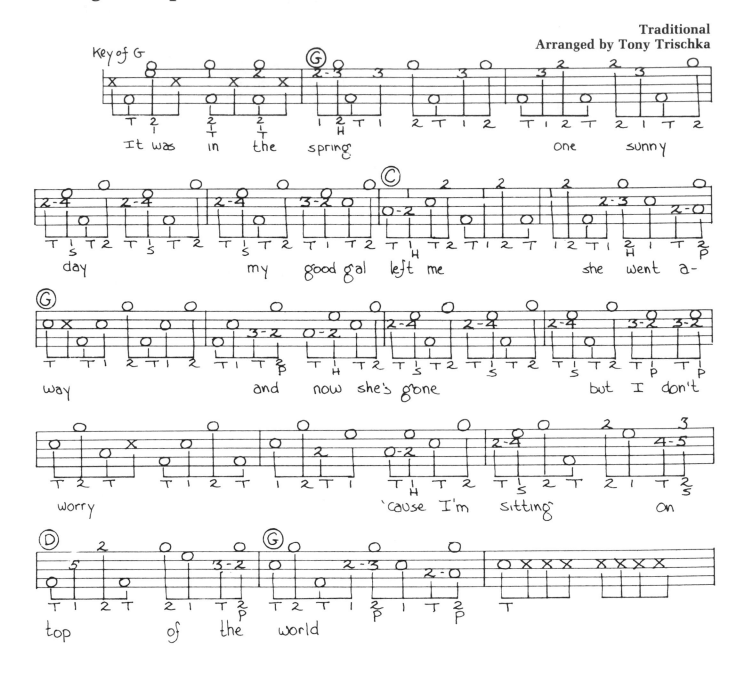

114

Don't Let Your Deal Go Down

Traditional
Arranged by Tony Trischka

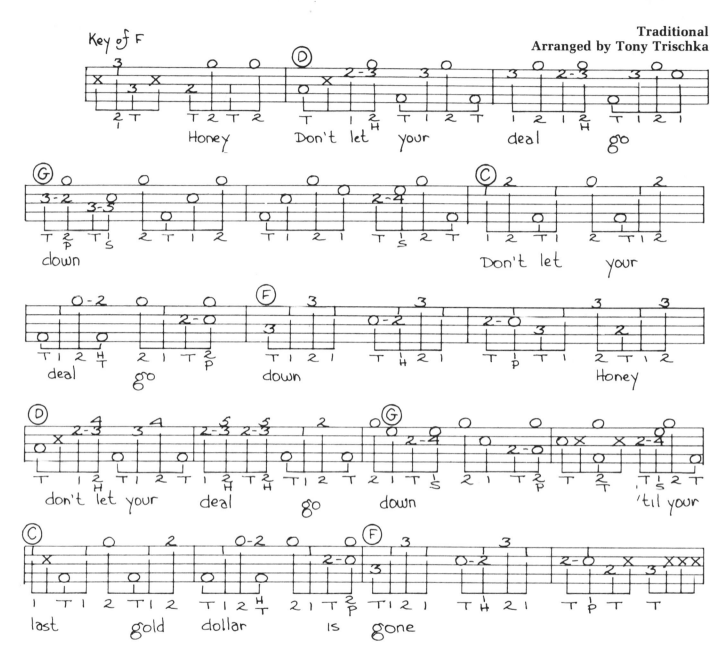

Dark Hollow

Traditional
Arranged by Tony Trischka

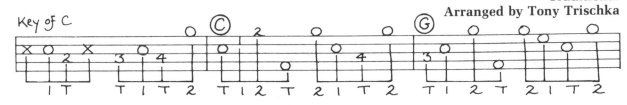

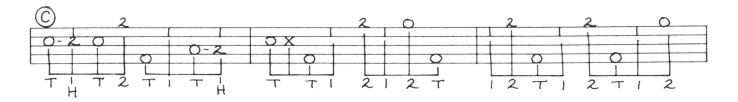

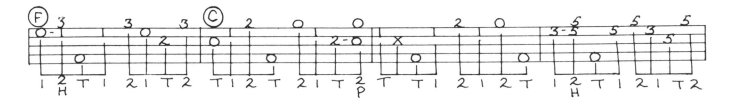

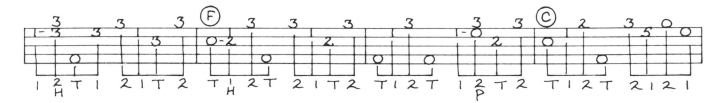

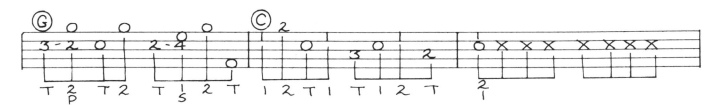

Cindy

Traditional
Arranged by Tony Trischka

Oh Susannah

Traditional
Arranged by Tony Trischka

Farewell Blues

(GCGBD)
Key of C

Schoebel, Mares and Rappolo

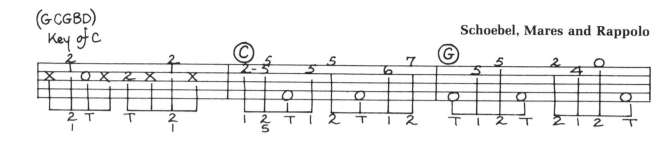

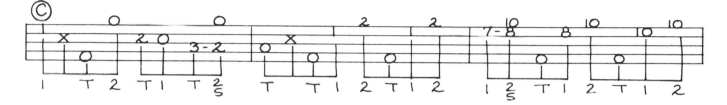

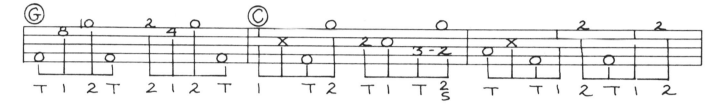

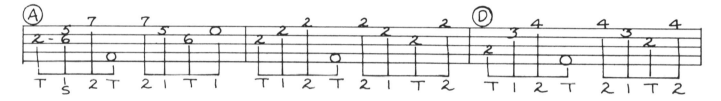

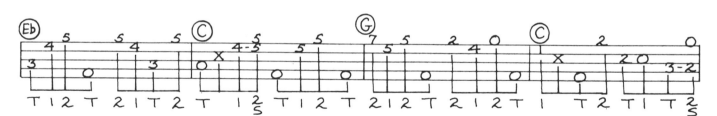

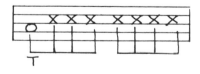

Flop Eared Mule

Traditional
Arranged by Tony Trischka

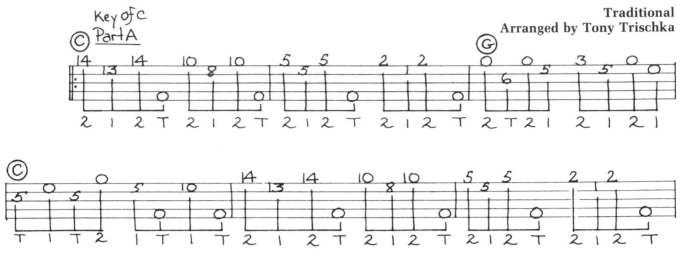

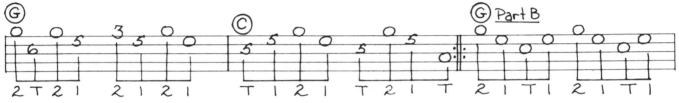

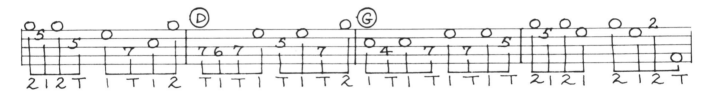

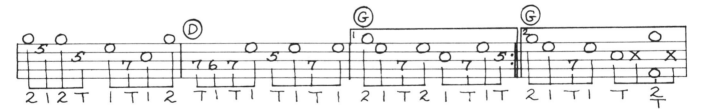

New River Train

Capo 5
Key of F

Traditional
Arranged by Alan Munde

From The White Brothers, "The New Kentucky Colonels" Rounder 0073

Bugle Call Rag

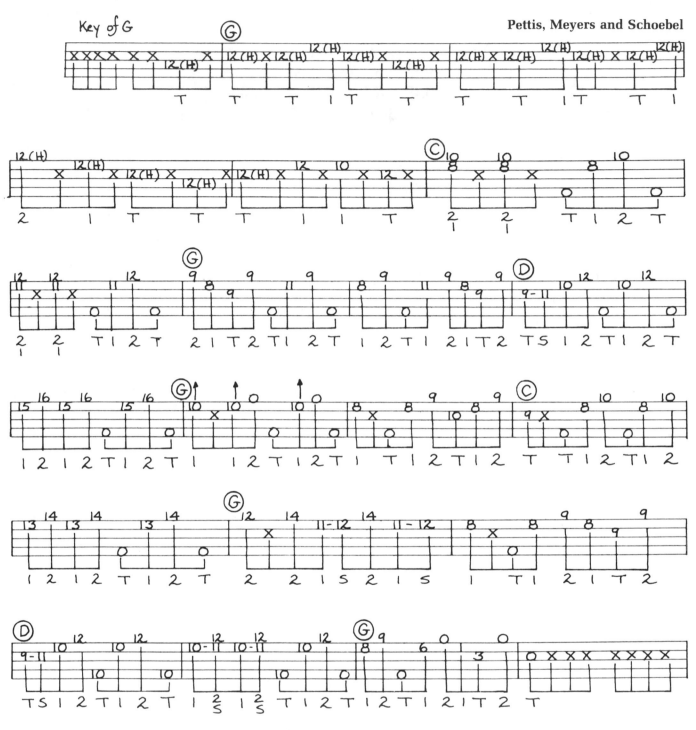

Sweet Dixie

Jimmy Martin and Bill Emerson

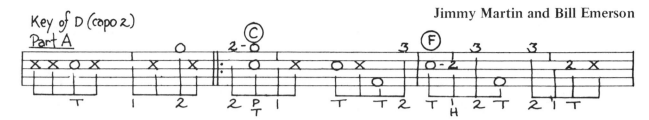

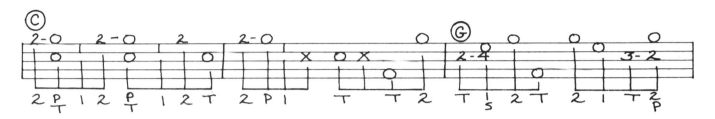

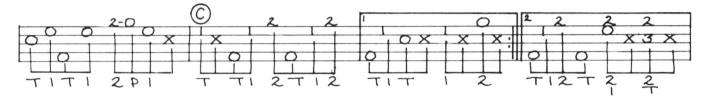

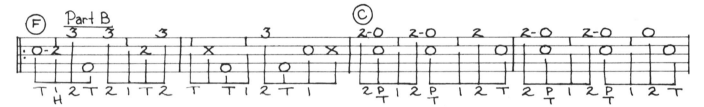

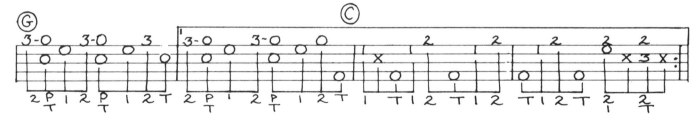

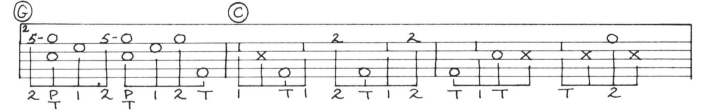

From Jimmy Martin's "Mr. Good 'n' Country" DL-4769

Colored Aristocracy

Traditional
Arranged by Tony Trischka

124

The Girl I Left Behind

Traditional
Arranged by Tony Trischka

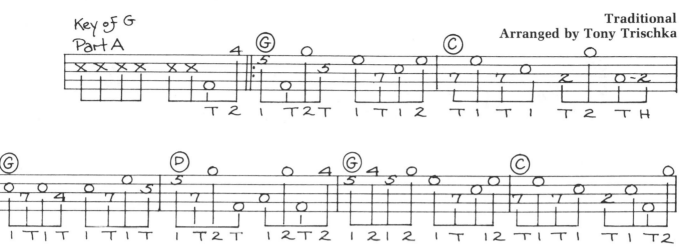

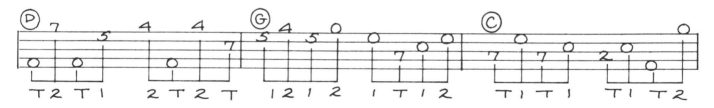

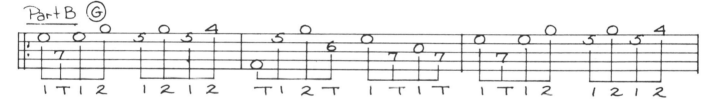

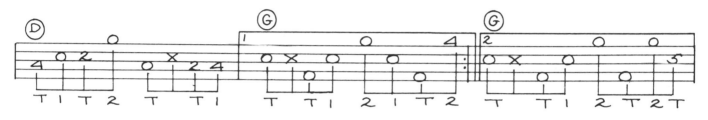

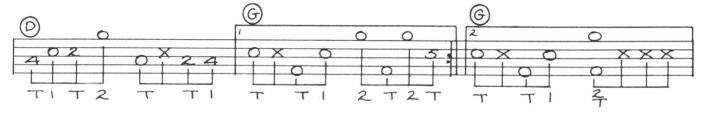

Little Maggie

Traditional
Arranged by Tony Trischka

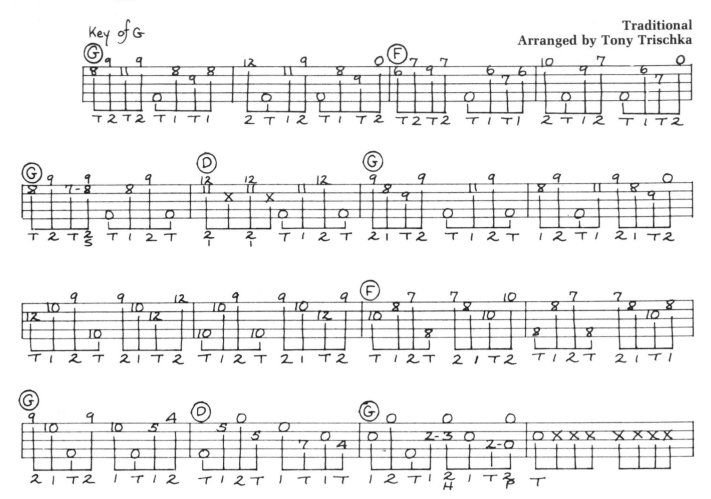

Hull's Victory

Traditional
Arranged by Hank Sapoznik and Bob Carlin

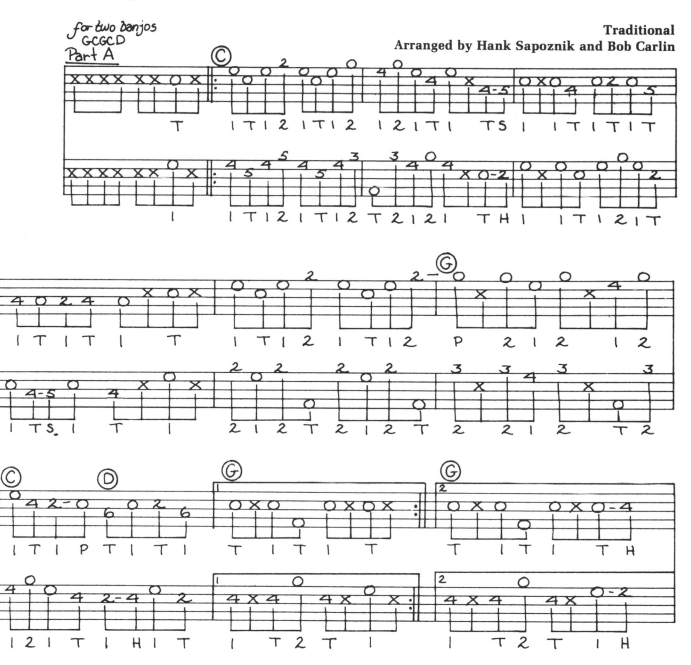

Part B

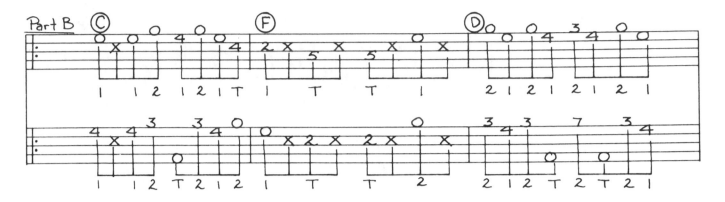

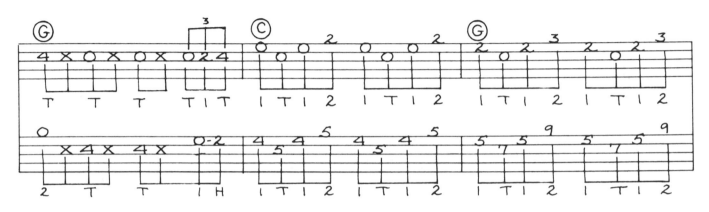

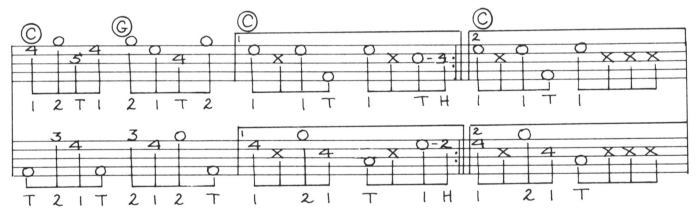

128

Hull's Victory

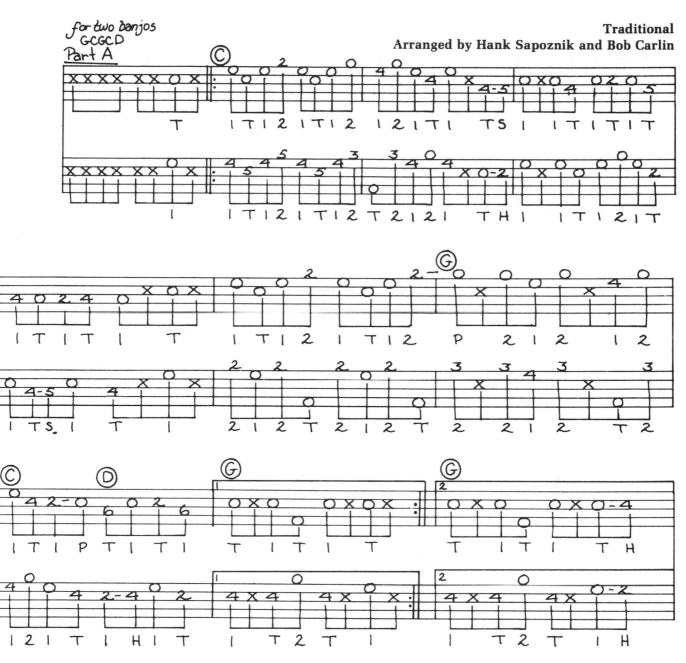

127

Part B

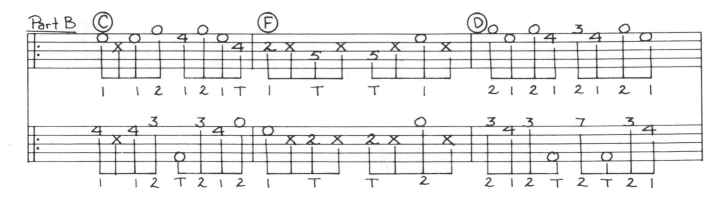

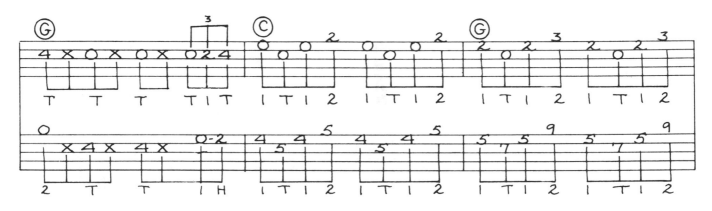

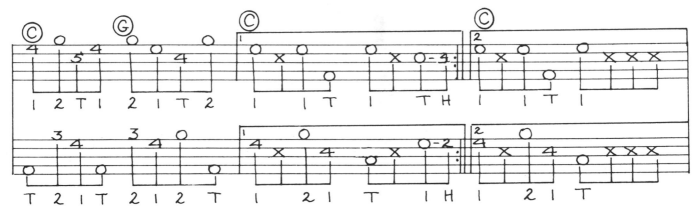

128

Blueberry Ripple

Peter Wernick

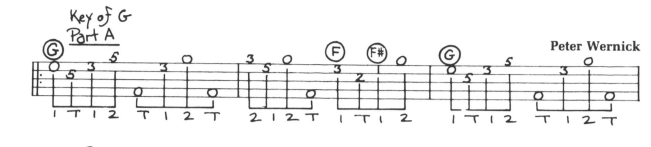

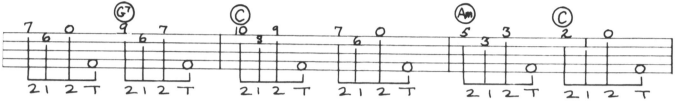

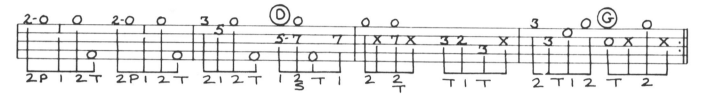

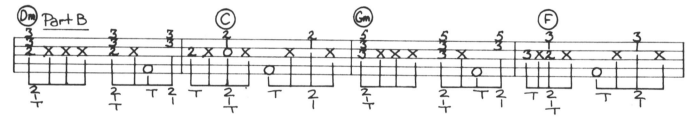

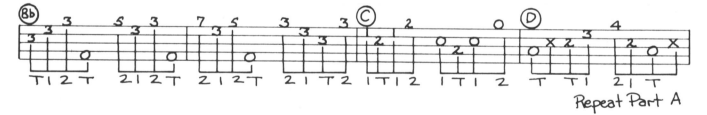

Repeat Part A

From Country Cooking and the Fiction Brothers, Flying Fish 019

Dill Pickle Rag

Traditional
Arranged by Tony Trischka

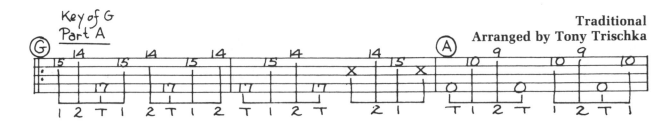

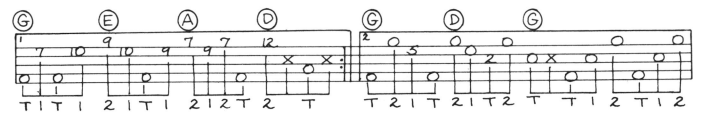

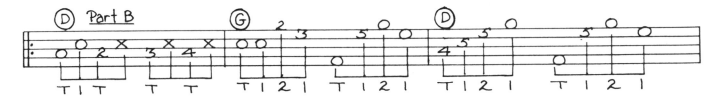

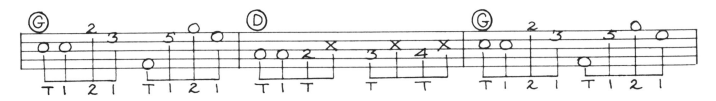

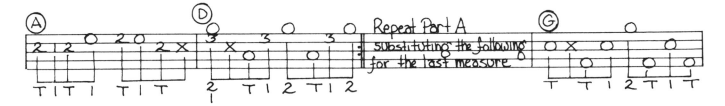

Oak Publications, 1977

Part C

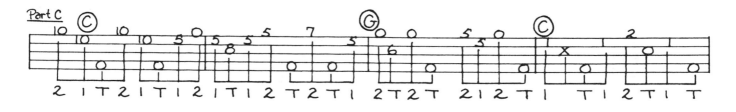

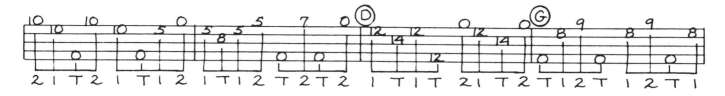

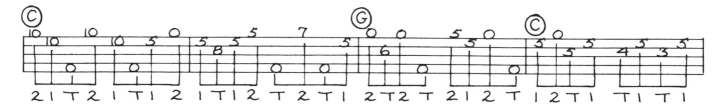

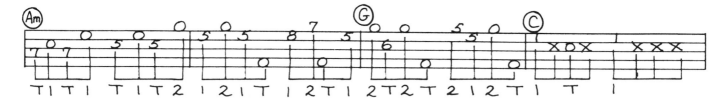

Golden Slippers

Traditional
Arranged by Tony Trischka

Key of G
Part A

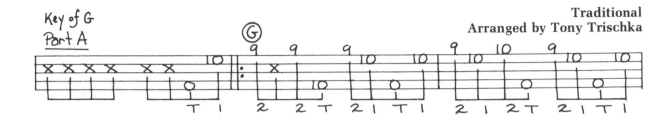

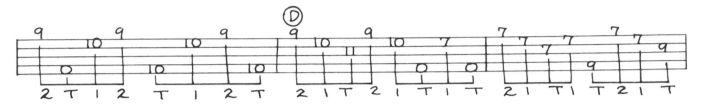

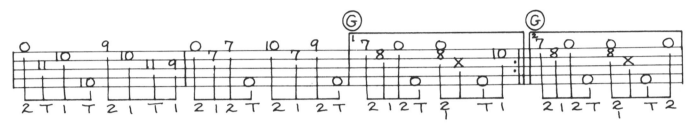

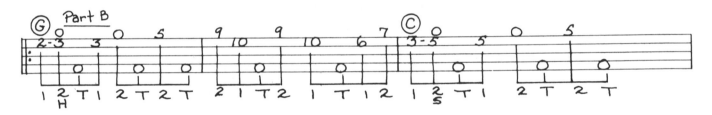

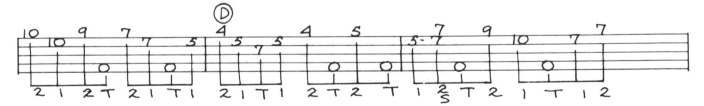

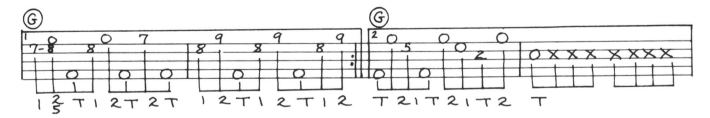

Orange Blossom Special

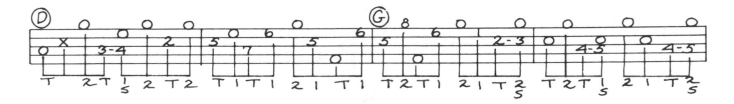

Part C

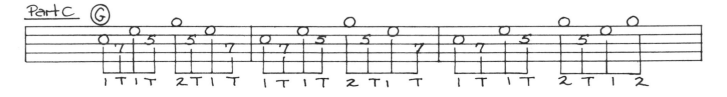

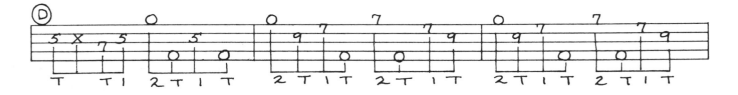

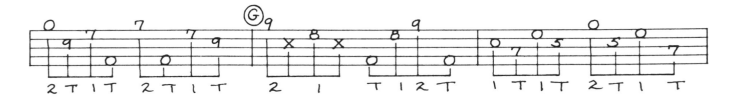

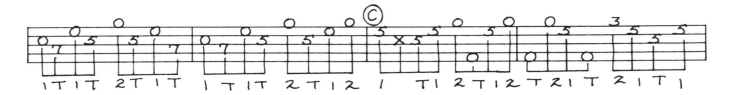

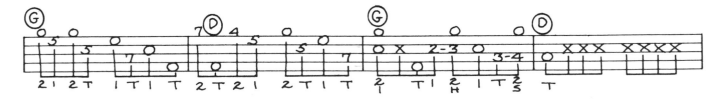

From Bean Blossom MCA 2-8002

Soddy Daisy

Key of G
Part A

Tony Trischka

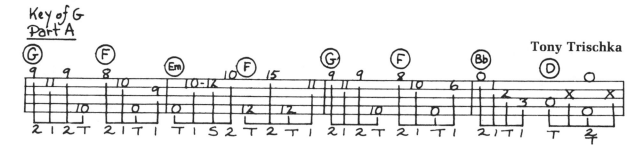

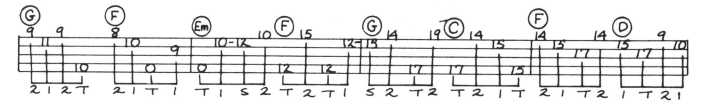

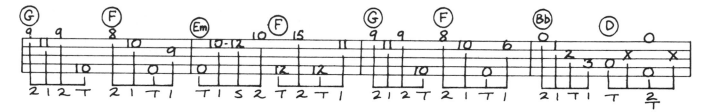

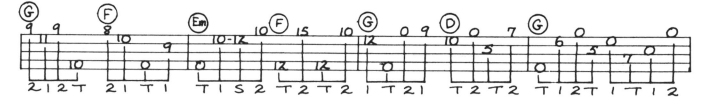

C Part B

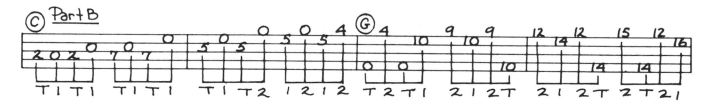

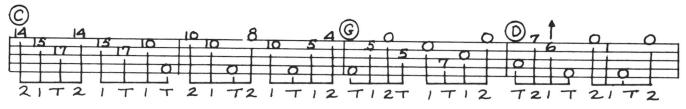

From Banjoland, Rounder Records 0087

Plastic Banana

David Nichtern

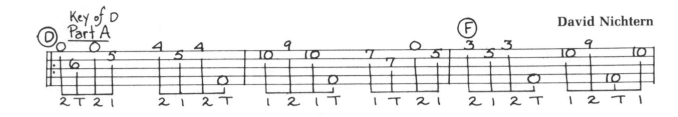

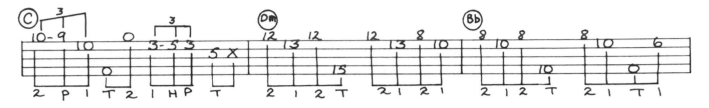

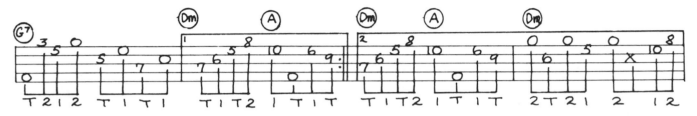

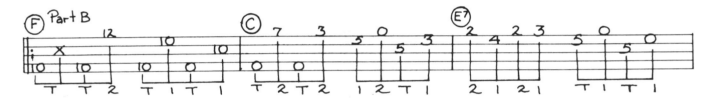

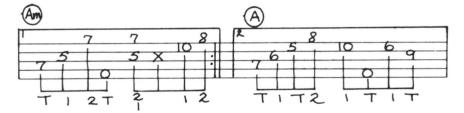

Bela's Dog

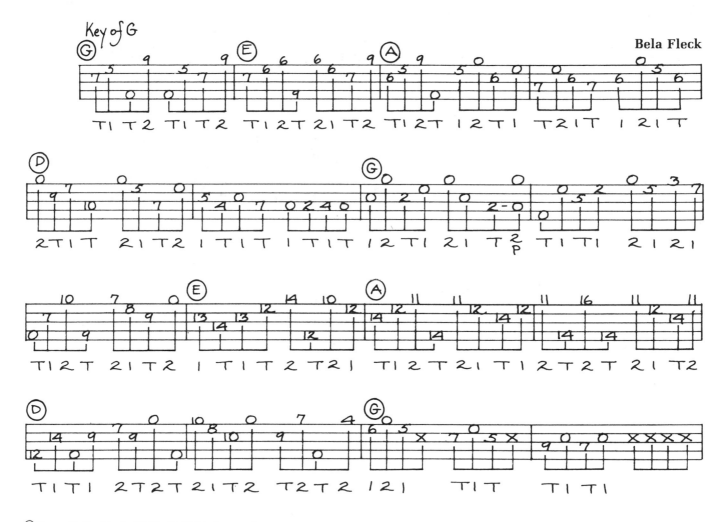

Appendix 1:
Some Notes on Music Theory

Scales and Chord Structure

Since this isn't really an instructional book, I've paid very little attention to music theory. However, if you really want to progress with your playing, you should know what you're doing theoretically. Enter scales and chords.

To begin with, there are seven letter names for notes: A, B, C, D, E, F and G. These are called *natural* notes. This is how they appear on the piano keyboard:

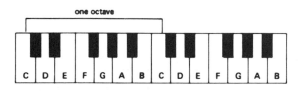

As you look at the keyboard, notice the interval between the first and second C notes. This span is called an *octave*. Every octave contains thirteen notes—eight naturals plus five other notes designated as either *sharps* (♯) or *flats* (♭), depending on the key you're playing in. These flats and sharps correspond to the black keys on the piano. To *flat* a note, drop down a half step (to the next lower fret on the banjo). To *sharp* a note, go up a half step. Thus, if your open first string is tuned to D, the first fret will be D♯, the second fret E, and so on.

By combining the thirteen notes of an octave in consecutive half step intervals, you'll create a *chromatic* scale. Out of these thirteen chromatic notes, there are eight which make up the major (do, re, mi) scale. In the key of C, for instance, the major scale is C, D, E, F, G, A, B and C. Now look at the piano keyboard. You'll notice that there is one whole step (two half steps) between C and D, and another whole step between D and E. This is followed by a half step from E to F, and then three more whole steps: F to G, G to A, and A to B. The scale concludes with a half step from B to C. This same pattern holds true for any major scale: whole step, whole step, half step, whole step, whole step, whole step, half step.

The following chart, constructed by Peter Wernick, indicates the eight basic notes in each of the twelve different scales.

	(do)	(re)	(mi)	(fa)	(sol)	(la)	(si)	(do)
Key	1	2	3	4	5	6	7	8
A	A	B	C♯	D	E	F♯	G♯	A
B	B	C♯	D♯	E	F♯	G♯	A♯	B
C	C	D	E	F	G	A	B	C
D	D	E	F♯	G	A	B	C♯	D
E	E	F♯	G♯	A	B	C♯	D♯	E
F	F	G	A	A♯	C	D	E	F
G	G	A	B	C	D	E	F♯	G
A♯	A♯	C	D	D♯	F	G	A	A♯
C♯	C♯	D♯	F	F♯	G♯	A♯	C	C♯
D♯	D♯	F	G	G♯	A♯	C	D	D♯
F♯	F♯	G♯	A♯	B	C♯	D♯	F	F♯
G♯	G♯	A♯	C	C♯	D♯	F	G	G♯

Now here are those same scales as they apply to the banjo. A number of them may seem useless to you at first, and you may ask yourself, "Why learn these?" Well, the answer is simple—to become more familiar with the fingerboard. That's the key to improving your improvisatory skills. As you increase your knowledge of the banjo neck, more varied musical possibilities will unfold before you. Unfortunately, I don't have the space to discuss the application of these scales here, so you'll have to experiment on your own. One further hint: you should practice these scales with a metronome. Start off slowly and then work up to the faster speeds as you gain proficiency. Remember, timing is all-important.

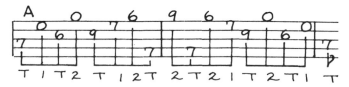

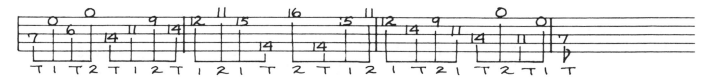

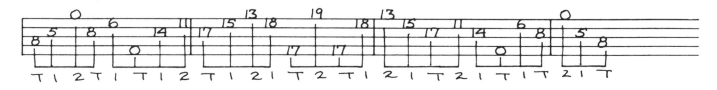

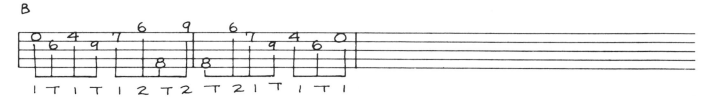

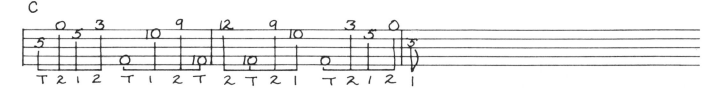

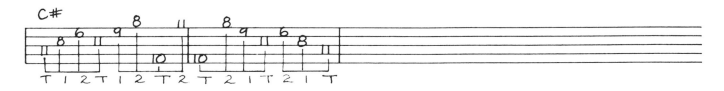

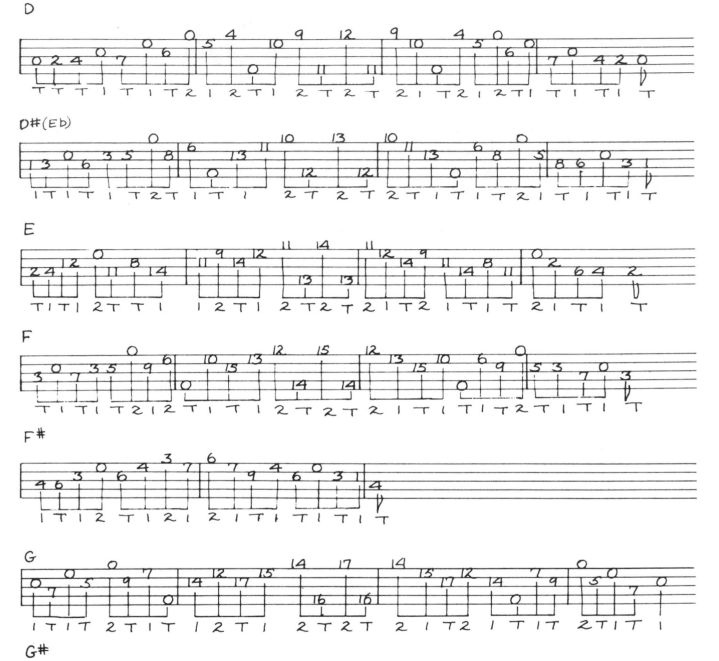

Referring again to the Peter Wernick chart, let's explore chord construction. All major *triads* (three note chords) are comprised of the 1, 3 and 5 notes. For example, a basic G chord consists of G, B and D; an A chord of A, C♯ and E. To get a minor chord, simply flat the 3 note a half step. A G minor chord would then consist of G, B♭ and D; an A minor chord of A, C and E.

Now I'm going to add certain notes to the basic triad form to create more colorful chords. For instance, a 6th chord is the sixth note of the scale added to a triad. This results in a jazzy sound found in the swing music of such people as Bob Wills and Hank Williams. Here are two different inversions of the 6th chord as they appear on the banjo. (Numbers on the frets indicate degrees of the scale.)

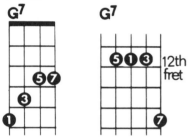

By moving the 6 note up a half step, you'll get a dominant 7th chord. This is actually the flat of the seventh degree of the scale. It's most commonly used in leading from a 1 chord to a 4 chord. Here are two inversions of the 7th chord:

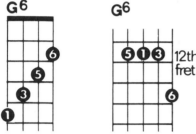

Raise the dominant 7th note up one half step and you'll find the major 7th which lends itself to a softer jazz feel. The G major 7th:

A 9th chord, as you may have guessed, adds the 9 note, which is actually the 2 note taken up one octave. A true 9th chord is made up of the 1, 3, 5, ♭7 and 9 notes. However, you can leave out one or two of these notes and still have the chord sound like a 9th. Here are two inversions of a G9 chord:

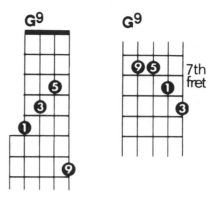

Finally, I want to discuss *augmented* and *diminished* chords. An augmented chord sharps the fifth degree of the scale a half step (1, 3, 5♯) and can be used as a transition between a 1 and 4 chord. Try this augmented G:

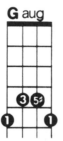

This chord is unique because it repeats every four frets in a different inversion. Thus an augmented G is the same as an augmented B which is the same as an augmented D♯, and so on. Try it for yourself.

Diminished chords also repeat, although every three frets instead of four. To get a diminished chord, flat the 3, 5 and dominant 7th notes a half step.

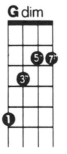

If some of these chords appeal to you, start by throwing them into your backup playing. Then as you get a better feel for their placement in a tune, break them down into individual notes and incorporate them into your leads. But first a warning: beware of bad taste! An augmented G9 chord may not sit very well in the middle of "The Little Girl and the Dreadful Snake." So experiment, but be discreet.

Appendix 2: Accessories

Fifth String Capo

As I mentioned earlier, you'll need a capo if you're going to play with other people. This gadget will make it much easier to work out of the less "open" keys, such as B. To get into the key of B, clasp your capo on the fourth fret. The capo should now cover the first four strings. Unfortunately, the fifth string will still be tuned down to G. This problem can be resolved by grabbing the fifth string peg and tuning the fifth string up four half steps—a dangerous proposition in terms of string whiplash. The alternative is to pick up a fifth string capo. There are two varieties of this animal—one that screws onto the side of the neck and a second that hammers into the fingerboard (H. O. railroad spikes). I recommend the spikes because they're less cumbersome when it comes to fretting the fifth string with your thumb. Don't try to put these in yourself since their placement in the neck requires very small drill bits and a certain degree of expertise. Your best bet is to go to an authorized repairman who's experienced in this line of work. He'll place the spikes (which can be picked up at most hobby stores) at the seventh and ninth frets so that you can play easily in the keys of A and B. (Tenth fret placement for the key of C is optional.)

Your other choice is the capo which screws onto the side of the neck. I avoid this type of device for two reasons: it tends to mark up the neck with screwholes and scraped finish, and the springwire which actually frets the string eventually becomes ineffectual. Nevertheless, it does have advantages in that you can capo your fifth string anywhere within a six or seven note range with the flick of a finger. Bill Monroe's banjo players find this to be a blessing since the man is known to kick off songs with little or no warning. For those of you who find yourself in a similar position, the Rick Shubb capo is the one to try. It's made of machined metal and though slightly on the bulky side, works very well.

Geared Fifth String Peg

In the good old days, you not only had to learn to play the banjo, you also had to struggle to keep it tuned. In short, tuning peg technology was in the Dark Ages. Today though, all sorts of precision tuning pegs are available, including the geared fifth.

Prior to the development of the geared fifth, fifth string pegs had only a 1:1 gear ratio. In other words, you would raise or lower the pitch of the string in direct proportion to the amount you turned the peg. As a result, it was easy to under- or overshoot the desired note on your first few tries. With the advent of the geared fifth string peg, however, much finer tuning accuracy became possible.

At present there are two recommended brands on the market: Kroll and Stewart-MacDonald. The Kroll peg has a 9:1 gear ratio—for every nine turns of the button there is one corresponding revolution of the shaft through which the string goes. The Stewart-MacDonald peg features a 4:1 gear ratio and differs from the Kroll in that it is a straight through peg, thus eliminating the shaft. Either brand does an excellent job. So pick one up today and say goodbye to tortured tuning forever.

Discography

In addition to instruction books and private lessons, your best learning aid is definitely records. You should be listening constantly. Get that banjo music in your head. In doing this you'll not only become clearer about the kinds of sounds you want to get out of your instrument, but you'll also have the experience of playing music you didn't know you knew. For instance: you get knocked out by a particular lick while listening to a J. D. Crowe album. Two weeks later you find that same lick crawling out of your subconscious, through your fingers and onto the strings. Moments like this make all the frustrations of learning worthwhile. So start accumulating those albums. Here's how to order:

Although an increasing number of record stores are stocking bluegrass in their bins, your best bets for good selection at reasonable prices are the following mail order outlets:

County Sales
Dept. T
Box 191
Floyd, Virginia 24091

Round-Up Records
P.O. Box 474
Somerville, Massachusetts 02144

Another company that imports some fine Japanese reissues of early *Flatt and Scruggs*, Monroe, and Stanley material is:

Southern Record Sales
5001 Reynard
La Crescenta, California 91214

They also carry a wide selection of the more readily available bluegrass albums. So write for their catalog.

Now here's a representative sampling of thirty-three banjo oriented records. I've divided them into three categories to parallel the structure of the history section in this book. These divisions aren't intended to be rigid because pigeonholing is, by nature, a subjective process. However, I've taken this approach to give you a better idea of what you're buying. Suffice it to say, the Mainstream section will list the players who are working primarily out of the Scruggs tradition, while the future section will consider those who lean more towards the experimental.

The Roots
William J. Ball—*The Classic Banjo of William J. Ball* Rounder 3005
Fred Van Eps and Vess L. Ossman—*Kings of the Ragtime Banjo* Yazoo 1044

Snuffy Jenkins—*Crazy Water Barndance* Rounder 0059
Charlie Poole—*The Legend of Charlie Poole* County 516
Harry Reser—*Banjo Crackerjax 1922–1930* Yazoo L-1048 (Although Reser was a 4–string player, his astounding technique should be of interest to you.)

The Mainstream
J. D. Crowe—*Rambling Boy* Lemco 525; *New South* Rounder 0044
Billy Edwards—with the *Shenandoah Cutups*—*Bluegrass Autumn* Revonah 904
Bill Emerson with *The Country Gentlemen*—Vanguard 79331
Raymond Fairchild—*King of the Smoky Mountain Banjo Players* Rural Rhythm 260
Lamar Grier with Bill Monroe—*Bluegrass Time* MCA 116
Jimmy Martin—*Big and Country Instrumentals* MCA 115 (with J. D. Crowe, Bill Emerson and Vic Jordan)
Earl Scruggs—*Flatt and Scruggs—The Golden Era* Rounder SS05. I highly recommend this album. They just don't make banjo music like this anymore.
Allen Shelton with Jim and Jesse—*Bluegrass Classics/Bluegrass Special* Epic CSP 12641
Don Stover and the *White Oak Mountain Boys* Rounder 0039
Chris Warner with the *Carroll County Ramblers* Adelphi AD 2006

The Future
Jimmy Arnold—*Strictly Arnold* Rebel 1538
Eddy Adcock with *The Country Gentlemen*—Vol. 4 *Going Back to the Blue Ridge Mountains* Folkways FTS-31031
Ben Eldridge with the *Seldom Scene—Recorded Live* Rebel 1547/48
John Hartford—*Nobody Knows What You Do* Flying Fish 028
Jack Hicks with Buck White—*Live at the Picking Parlor* County 760
Vic Jordan—*Pickaway* API 1027
Courtney Johnson with the *Newgrass Revival—When the Storm Is Over* Flying Fish 032
Bill Keith—*Something Auld, Something Newgrass, Something Borrowed, Something Bluegrass* Rounder RB1
Bill Knopf—*On Banjo* American Heritage 401-524
Raymond McLain with the *McLain Family Band—Country Life* CLR 4
Sue Monick—*Melting Pots* Adelphi AD 4107
Alan Munde—*Banjo Sandwich* Ridge Runner RRR-0001 with *Poor Richard's Almanac*—American Heritage 401-255
Tony Trischka—*Heartlands* Rounder 0062; *Bluegrass Light* Rounder 0048; *Banjoland,* Rounder 0087
Eric Weissberg—*Dueling Banjos* Warner Brothers 2683
Peter Wernick with *Country Cooking—Country Cooking* 0006; *Barrel of Fun* Rounder 0033

Bibliography

With every passing year more and more banjo books find their way to market. Although they all have something to offer, I think you'll be able to realize the highest gains from the following:

Bluegrass Banjo by Peter Wernick (Oak Publications). This book takes you from beginning to advanced with attention to all details in between. Highly recommended.

Earl Scruggs and the Five String Banjo by Earl Scruggs (Peer). You can do no better than to learn Earl's breaks note for note and here they are. Also highly recommended.

Melodic Banjo by Tony Trischka (Oak). A complete guide to the melodic style featuring interviews with and music of Bill Keith, Bobby Thompson, Alan Munde, etc. At the risk of honking my own horn, I'll recommend this too.

Hot Licks and Fiddle Tunes for the Bluegrass Banjo Player by Bill Knopf (Chappell Music). The first book of its kind to feature a panorama of fancy scales, licks and endings to spice up your playing. A veritable smorgasbord of musical delight. This fine volume also contains twelve fiddle tunes. Not to be missed.

5-String Banjo Fiddle Tunes (Mel Bay). An explanation of technique and a collection of songs in the melodic style. A good way to expand your repertoire.

Magazines

As I'm writing this there are three major bluegrass magazines on the market:

Bluegrass Unlimited
Box 111
Broad Run, Virginia 22014

Pickin'
46 Ford Road
Denville, New Jersey 07834

Banjo Newsletter
1310 Hawkins Lane
Annapolis, Maryland 21401

Although other periodicals come and go, these three have demonstrated a solid capacity for survival (*Bluegrass Unlimited* has been publishing since 1965). For our purposes, *Banjo Newsletter* should be of greatest interest. Every month it contains interviews, reviews and tablature dealing not only with bluegrass but also old time pickers. If you can only afford to subscribe to one of the above, this is the one.